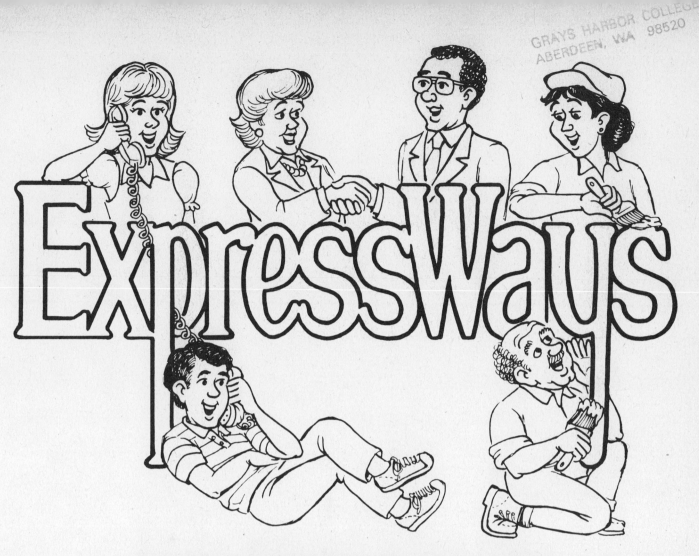

ExpressWays

COMPANION WORKBOOK

3A

Steven J. Molinsky · Bill Bliss

Contributing Authors

Susan Siegel
Carol Piñeiro

PRENTICE HALL REGENTS, Englewood Cliffs, NJ 07632

Editorial/production supervision and
   interior design: Elaine Price
Development: Ellen Lehrburger
Cover design: Lundgren Graphics Ltd.
Manufacturing buyer: Margaret Rizzi
Page layout: Audrey Kopciak and Karen Noferi

Cover Drawing by Gabriel Polonsky

ISBN 0-13-298340-0 01

Prentice-Hall International (UK) Limited, *London*
Prentice-Hall of Australia Pty. Limited, *Sydney*
Prentice-Hall Canada Inc., *Toronto*
Prentice-Hall Hispanoamericana, S.A., *Mexico*
Prentice-Hall of India Private Limited, *New Delhi*
Prentice-Hall of Japan, Inc., *Tokyo*
Prentice-Hall of Southeast Asia Pte. Ltd., *Singapore*
Editora Prentice-Hall do Brasil, Ltda., *Rio de Janeiro*

CONTENTS

Chapter	Page
1	1
2	10
3	19
4	30
5	38
6	48
7	59
8	70
9	79

Tape Scripts for Listening
Exercises 91

Who	Why	When
What	Where	How (long)

Peter van Dyke is at your employment agency. You are the interviewer. Write an appropriate question for each response Peter gives.

1. A. _What's your name?_

   B. My name is Peter van Dyke.

2. A. _Where are you from?_

   B. I'm from Holland.

3. A. _what do you do._

   B. I'm an illustrator.

4. A. _How long have you worked there?_

   B. For five years.

5. A. _where do you work?_

   B. At the Leiden Design Company in Amsterdam.

6. A. _why did you move to the U.S.?_

   B. I decided to move to the United States because I wanted some overseas experience.

7. A. _When do you work._

   B. I want to start working as soon as possible.

8. A. _who can you call?_

   B. You can call my previous employer, Mr. Haviland, for a recommendation.

   A. Okay. I'll see what I can do.

   B. Thank you very much. I look forward to hearing from you.

Listen and circle the best response to Speaker A.

Example   You will hear: I don't think we've met. My name is Joe.

               Answer: a. How about you, Joe?
                                b. What about you, Joe?
                                ⓒ Nice to meet you, Joe.

1.   a.   Fine, thanks.
     ⓑ   All right.
     c.   I'm a lawyer.

2.   a.   I'm fine.
     b.   Nice to meet you.
     ⓒ   I'm a computer engineer.

3.   a.   New York.
     b.   2D.
     ⓒ   Yes, I do.

4.   a.   I've been studying.
     ⓑ   In Boston.
     c.   Two months.

5.   a.   I'm a student.
     ⓑ   Math.
     c.   I'm an accountant.

6.   a.   I like jazz.
     b.   Yes, I like it.
     ⓒ   Yes, I do.

7.   a.   He's fine.
     b.   Next month.
     ⓒ   He's playing in his room.

8.   a.   The blue ones.
     b.   Mine.
     ⓒ   I like the brown shoes.

FUNCTIONS   Student Course Book pp. 2–3

For each of the following dialogs, circle the appropriate line for Speaker B.

1.   A.   I don't think we've met. I'm Carmen.
     B.   a.   How about you?
           ⓑ   How do you do?
           c.   What about you?

2.   A.   My name is Jane.
     B.   ⓐ   And you?
           b.   Hello. My name is Paul.
           c.   I'm glad.

3.   A.   Nice to meet you. What do you do?
     B.   a.   I'm fine, thanks.
           b.   I'm pleased to meet you.
           ⓒ   I'm a lawyer.

4.   A.   I'm from Texas. What about you?
     B.   a.   I'm a doctor.
           ⓑ   I'm from Massachusetts.
           c.   I'm happy to meet you.

5.   A.   I'm pleased to meet you.
     B.   ⓐ   Nice meeting you, too.
           b.   How about you?
           c.   What about you?

6.   A.   I'm a History major. And you?
     B.   ⓐ   My major is Chemistry.
           b.   I'm Dave.
           c.   Hi.

7.   A.   What kind of work do you do?
     B.   a.   I'm very busy.
           b.   Every day.
           ⓒ   I'm a teacher.

8.   A.   I like skiing. What about you?
     B.   a.   Yes.
           ⓑ   I like it, too.
           c.   I'm happy.

Listen and circle the best answer.

Example   You will hear: A.   Hi, John. I haven't seen you in a long time.
                              B.   I know. How have you been, Paul?

              Answer: ⓐ John and Paul are old friends.
                             b. John and Paul are meeting for the first time.
                             c. John asked Paul what time it was.

1. a. They are good friends.
    b. This is the first time they've met.
    ⓒ Sam thinks he has met Dr. Jones before.

2. a. Tom thinks Sally is nice.
    b. Sally has met Tom before.
    c. Sally and Tom are both happy to meet each other.

3. a. Kim wants to go to Spain.
    ⓑ Kim wants to know where Luis is from.
    c. Kim wants to know how Luis is feeling.

4. a. The accountant asked the engineer about his job.
    b. The engineer wants to be an accountant.
    c. The accountant asked about the engineer's health.

5. a. Joan's friend has been studying for a year.
    ⓑ Joan has been studying for a year.
    c. Joan wants to study for one more year.

6. a. Peter is getting married.
    b. Arthur is getting married.
    ⓒ Peter asked Arthur where he was going.

7. a. Lucy doesn't like rock and roll.
    ⓑ Lucy is kind.
    c. Rock and roll is Lucy's favorite music.

8. a. Carol doesn't have anything to do until Friday.
    b. Carol has to write a paper by Friday.
    ⓒ Carol's friend doesn't know what to do on Friday.

9. a. Bob's school is tall.
    ⓑ Bob is tall.
    c. Bob lives in a tall building.

10. a. Ruth is going to see Martha.
    b. Ruth is leaving Martha's office.
    ⓒ Martha is asking Ruth where she is going.

Over the years, Americans have greeted each other in a variety of ways. Many years ago, native Americans raised one hand as a sign of peace and friendship and said "How!", a greeting from the Sioux language. Early colonists who came to the New World seeking religious freedom often greeted each other with Biblical phrases such as "Peace be to you." Other groups brought with them courtly European gestures such as bowing and curtsying. The greater the status of the person greeted, the deeper the bow or curtsy. In informal situations, men shook hands with each other and kissed the hands of women. As time passed, the bow evolved into a simple tip of the hat and the curtsy became a nod of the head. "How do you do?" was shortened to "Howdy," a greeting still heard in some parts of the United States today. In recent times, the handshake has become the common gesture of greeting for both men and women.

When Americans shake hands, they usually stand about two feet apart. If they are friends, they may also pat each other on the shoulder or arm. Women sometimes exchange a kiss on the cheek or a quick hug.

The greeting "Hi, how are you?" has become a routine way of saying hello and is not usually meant as a question about how the other person is feeling. The response "Fine, thanks" is very typical and does not necessarily convey any real information.

It is important to note that Americans consider a "firm handshake" the trademark of a strong character. People think that many virtues of manhood and womanhood are conveyed in the strength of the handshake and that conversely, a weak handshake implies a weak character. Americans often form a first impression about people by the way they shake hands.

I. Circle the best answer.

1. The way Americans greet each other today depends on
   a. how well they know each other.
   b. the early colonists.
   c. a "firm handshake."

2. When people say, "Hi, how are you?" they are usually
   a. asking about someone's health.
   b. shaking hands.
   c. greeting someone.

3. Greetings vary
   a. according to first impressions.
   b. through time.
   c. about two feet apart.

4. The strength of a person's handshake conveys
   a. politeness.
   b. virtues and vices.
   c. strength of character.

5. Another title for this passage would be
   a. Greetings Past and Present.
   b. Introductions and Greetings.
   c. Ethnic Greetings.

II. Match the words in the first column with their meanings in the second column.

a. variety _baricdad_

b. raise _levantar_

c. seeking

d. status

e. evolved

f. gesture

g. routine _indicar_

h. convey _Trosportar_

i. trademark

j. implies

1. __c__ looking for

2. _____ position, rank

3. __e__ developed gradually

4. _____ transmit

5. __a__ different kinds

6. _____ indicates indirectly

7. _____ symbol

8. _____ lift

9. _____ normal, commonplace

10. _____ movement of some part of the body

WRITING   Student Course Book p. 4

First impressions are important, but different people have different standards for judging others the first time they meet. The following is a list of characteristics people might use to form their impressions of others. Check *Important* or *Not Important* according to whether you would consider the following characteristics when forming your "first impression" of somebody you have just met.

		Important	Not Important
1.	Firm handshake	1. _____	_____
2.	Confident walk	2. _____	_____
3.	Humble demeanor	3. _____	_____
4.	Well-groomed appearance	4. _____	_____
5.	Honest, open face	5. _____	_____
6.	Good "eye contact"	6. _____	_____
7.	Friendly smile	7. _____	_____
8.	Quiet, serious attitude	8. _____	_____
9.	Air of self-assurance	9. _____	_____
10.	Attractive features	10. _____	_____
11.	Sense of humor	11. _____	_____
12.	Interesting conversationalist	12. _____	_____
13.	Graduate of an important university	13. _____	_____
14.	Member of a prominent family	14. _____	_____
15.	Good position in a company	15. _____	_____

Write a paragraph about a person who you feel would make a good first impression.

Write a negative question and response for each of the following situations.

1. You and a friend are in line for a movie. You suddenly begin to think that you've seen the movie before.

   A. _Haven't we seen this movie before?_

   B. No, _we haven't_.

2. You're at a friend's house. You think your friend is going to watch the news.

   A. _____

   B. No, _____.

3. You and your roommate want to make lunch. You think you bought some tuna fish last week.

   A. _____

   B. Yes, _____.

4. You and a friend are on a bicycle trip. You think you're on the wrong road.

   A. _____

   B. No, _____.

5. You meet someone at a party. You think you've met the person before.

   A. _____

   B. No, _____.

6. You meet someone on the subway. You think he's your brother's friend from high school.

   A. _____

   B. Yes, _____.

7. You and a group of friends are on an exhausting hike. You've already hiked fifteen miles, and you think you've hiked long enough.

   A. _____

   B. Yes, _____.

Circle the best answer.

1. Ernest Hemingway was a famous author. He was
   - a. the one who
   - b. the one whose
   - c. the one which

   wrote *The Sun Also Rises*.

2. Romeo and Juliet are famous Shakespearean characters. They are
   - a. the ones who
   - b. the one whose
   - c. the ones whose

   parents disapproved of their love.

3. Thomas Edison was an inventor. He was
   - a. the one that
   - b. the one who
   - c. the one whose

   creative ideas led to the invention of the light bulb.

4. Degas, Monet, and Renoir were French artists. They were some of
   - a. the one whose
   - b. the ones whose
   - c. the ones who

   began the movement called Impressionism.

5. Beethoven was a German composer. He was
   - a. the one who
   - b. the ones which
   - c. the one which

   composed "Für Elise."

6. Sally Ride is an astronaut. She is
   - a. the one whose
   - b. the one who
   - c. the one that

   flight made history because she was the first American woman to travel in space.

7. Albert Einstein was a physicist. His theories were
   - a. the ones who
   - b. the ones which
   - c. the one that

   explained the idea of gravitational forces.

8. Muhammad Ali was a boxer. He is
   - a. the one whose
   - b. the one that
   - c. the ones who

   was world heavyweight champion from 1964–1967.

9. Abraham Lincoln was a U.S. president. He was
   - a. the one whom
   - b. the one which
   - c. the one who

   freed the slaves.

10. "Peanuts" is a comic strip. It is
    - a. the one that
    - b. the one who
    - c. the one whose

    features a round-faced boy named Charlie Brown and his dog named Snoopy.

Match the words in the first column with their meanings in the second column.

a.	head	1. _____	be infatuated with
b.	retire	2. _____	stop working because of age
c.	baby-sit	3. _____	meet accidentally
d.	scare	4. _____	take care of children
e.	break down	5. _____	frighten
f.	get loose	6. _____	boyfriend or girlfriend
g.	every once in a while	7. _____	break away from, run away
h.	bump into, run into	8. _____	stop running
i.	sweetheart	9. _____	occasionally
j.	have a crush on	10. _____	director

GRAMMAR CHECK: *Verb Tenses*

Circle the best answer.

1. I _____ my cousin for lunch today.
   a. meet
   b. met
   c. would meet

2. I _____ him every once in a while.
   a. was running into
   b. am running to
   c. run into

3. David _____ in San Francisco when he was younger.
   a. lives
   b. is living
   c. used to live

4. My grandparents _____ usually visit us on Sundays when I was a child.
   a. was
   b. would
   c. did

5. _____ a good time at the party?
   a. Had you
   b. Did you have
   c. Haven't you

6. I _____ very athletic, but I'm not any more.
   a. am
   b. used to be
   c. would be

7. Where _____ after the lecture the other night?
   a. you went
   b. were you go
   c. did you go

8. Who _____ the head of the department?
   a. is
   b. does
   c. be

For each of the following dialogs, circle the most appropriate line for Speaker A.

1. A. ⓐ How's it going?
      b. Don't I know you from somewhere?
      c. Did she have anything to say?
   B. All right.

2. A. a. I guess I made a mistake.
      b. I don't think I remember her.
      c. We just talked for a minute.
   B. Oh, sure you do!

3. A. a. It was really good to see you again.
      b. Now I remember her.
      c. You must have me confused with somebody else.
   B. Excuse me.

4. A. a. Guess who I saw yesterday!
      b. How is she?
      c. How are you?
   B. Who?

5. A. a. Sure.
      b. Let me introduce you to my friend Susan.
      c. Don't I know you from somewhere?
   B. No, I don't think so.

6. A. a. I don't think I remember her.
      b. You won't believe who I bumped into the other day!
      c. She's the one who taught Economics at the University.
   B. Oh, of course.

7. A. a. How are you doing?
      b. I'd like you to meet my fiancé, Robert Smith.
      c. Pretty good.
   B. Nice to meet you.

8. A. a. Did they have anything to say?
      b. We just talked for a minute.
      c. They don't look very well.
   B. Not really.

9. A. a. Oh, I'm sorry.
      b. How are things?
      c. Her old car would always break down in bad weather.
   B. Not bad.

10. A. a. Guess who I saw this morning!
       b. Aren't you a reporter from the local newspaper?
       c. It was great to see him again.
    B. No, I'm afraid not.

2

Write a sentence using a passive construction for each situation.

1. IBM just offered me a job.

   I was just offered a job by IBM.

2. My father built that house.

   _____

3. A famous chef is preparing the food for the diplomats.

   _____

4. Christian Dior is going to design my wedding gown.

   _____

5. Vincent van Gogh painted that painting.

   _____

6. The principal makes announcements every Monday morning.

   _____

7. A calligrapher addressed the invitations.

   _____

8. A wonderful florist will decorate the church.

   _____

9. The President had signed the bill just before he left office.

   _____

10. Santa Claus is ringing the bells in front of the department store.

    _____

11. Johnny's mother ties his shoes every morning.

    _____

12. The National Science Foundation will give Tom a grant to do research.

    _____

Listen and circle the answer that is *closest in meaning* to the sentence you have heard.

Example   You will hear: I have some good news!

              Answer: a.   The news was good today.
                         (b.)   I have something good to tell you.
                         c.   I have something new to tell you.

1. a. That's wonderful!
   b. I agree.
   c. That's right.

2. a. Are you sick?
   b. I'm sure you're happy.
   c. That's too bad.

3. a. I was on the news.
   b. I'm afraid.
   c. Something bad has happened.

4. a. What happened?
   b. I'm happy for you.
   c. I didn't hear that.

5. a. You must be staying here.
   b. That's a shame.
   c. I'm sure you're happy.

6. a. That's wonderful!
   b. What a pity!
   c. That's a shame!

7. a. That's too bad.
   b. I forgive you.
   c. I didn't hear that.

8. a. You must be thrilled.
   b. You must sit up.
   c. I think you're unhappy about that.

Listen and circle the best response to Speaker A.

Example   You will hear: I have some bad news.

              Answer: (a.)   Oh? What is it?
                         b.   Well, congratulations!
                         c.   That's fantastic!

1. a. Oh, that's a pity!
   b. Really? What a shame!
   c. Really? Congratulations!

2. a. Oh, I'm sorry to hear that.
   b. What a thrill!
   c. I'm so pleased!

3. a. What a shame!
   b. That's exciting!
   c. I'm sorry to hear that.

4. a. Oh, that's too bad!
   b. I'm very happy to hear that.
   c. You must be ecstatic!

5. a. That's exciting!
   b. I'm very pleased.
   c. That's a shame.

6. a. I'm thrilled for you.
   b. I'm very sorry.
   c. You did?

7. a. You must be thrilled.
   b. I'm afraid so.
   c. That's terrible!

8. a. That's exciting!
   b. That's too bad!
   c. I'm very happy to hear that.

Write an appropriate deduction for the situations below using one of the following adjectives.

patient	intelligent	honest
strict	short-tempered	sick
articulate	upset	lonely

1. The babysitter spent three hours getting the baby to stop crying.

    <u>She must be very patient.</u>

2. Mrs. Lyman wrote a brilliant analysis of the problem.

    _____

3. Simon went to the hospital yesterday.

    _____

4. I used to live with three roommates, but they all moved out.

    _____

5. Mr. Wilson wouldn't let his class leave until exactly 3:00 P.M.

    _____

6. Sally's cat ran away.

    _____

7. My cousin George fights with people very often.

    _____

8. The President of the United States spoke clearly and concisely. She gave an excellent speech.

    _____

9. Jennifer found a twenty-dollar bill and immediately brought it to the police station.

    _____

Circle the best answer.

1. Have you _____ your neighbor
   recently?
   a. seen
   b. been
   c. talked

2. Have you _____ your cousin
   lately?
   a. heard from
   b. run
   c. talked

3. How _____ she?
   a. is doing
   b. has been
   c. is

4. She's not _____.
   a. lately
   b. very
   c. well

5. That's too _____.
   a. pity
   b. bad
   c. great

6. Next time you see her, _____.
   a. regard her
   b. tell her my regards
   c. tell her I say hello

7. I _____ Ralph yesterday.
   a. ran into
   b. been in touch with
   c. seen

8. How _____ he been?
   a. has
   b. is
   c. was

9. He _____.
   a. wonderful
   b. has been all right
   c. fine

10. That's _____!
    a. well
    b. ecstatic
    c. fantastic

Circle the best answer.

1. _____ from your boyfriend
   lately?
   a. Did you hear
   b. Have you heard
   c. Are you hearing

2. Yes, I _____ from him yesterday.
   a. heard
   b. was hearing
   c. have heard

3. How _____ now?
   a. has he done
   b. was he doing
   c. is he doing

4. Oh, he's fine. He _____ the
   football team last week.
   a. is joining
   b. has joining
   c. joined

5. That's great. Next time you
   _____ him, send him my
   regards.
   a. will see
   b. saw
   c. see

6. _____ to do that next time we go
   out.
   a. I'm sure
   b. Are you sure
   c. I'll be sure

7. _____ to your friend Margaret
   lately?
   a. Had you spoken
   b. Have you spoken
   c. Will you speak

(continued)

8. Yes, as a matter of fact I _____ to her two days ago.
   a. will speak
   b. have spoken
   c. spoke

9. She isn't very well. She _____ her leg skiing last week.
   a. broke
   b. break
   c. has broken

10. That's too bad! Please _____ my regards.
    a. sending her
    b. tell to her
    c. send her

11. Have you _____ in touch with Stella recently?
    a. be
    b. been
    c. were

12. Yes. She's just _____ president of the class.
    a. be chose
    b. chosen
    c. been chosen

13. Next time you see her, _____.
    a. tell her I thought her
    b. tell I'm thinking of her
    c. tell her I'm thinking of her

VOCABULARY   Student Course Book p. 14

I. Circle the word that does not relate to the rest of the words in the group.

1. *height*   a. long   b. short   c. tall   d. average

2. *weight*   a. thin   b. heavy   c. fat   d. thick

3. *hair*   a. curly   b. wavy   c. heavy   d. straight

4. *hair color*   a. black   b. blond   c. gray   d. yellow

5. *additional features*   a. beard   b. glasses   c. watch   d. mustache

II. Combine the following sentences.

1. The superintendent is a fat man. He has curly black hair.

   <u>The superintendent is a fat man with curly black hair.</u>

2. Our accountant is a short man. He has gray hair and a beard.

   _____

3. My boss is a thin woman. She has brown hair and a nice smile.

   _____

4. Our principal is a heavy man. He has a receding hairline and a mustache.

   _____

Underline the correct answer.

1. A. Have you heard anything about our new science teacher?
   B. Yes. People say she's patient (<u>and</u> / but) kind.

2. A. What have you heard about our new history teacher?
   B. Everybody tells me she's nice (and / but) boring.

3. A. What have you heard about the new supervisor?
   B. They say he's intelligent (and / but) not very friendly.

4. A. Have you heard anything else about him?
   B. Well, word has it that he's short-tempered (and / but) inconsiderate.

5. A. Do you know anything about Linda's new boyfriend?
   B. Yes. Everybody tells me he's interesting (and / but) conceited.

6. A. What have you heard about the new Walt Disney film?
   B. People say it's educational (and / but) enjoyable.

7. A. I've heard that the new kid up the block is mean (and /but) selfish.
   B. Everybody at school tells me that he's lazy (and / but) inconsiderate.

8. A. What have you heard about our new boss?
   B. They say he's friendly (and / but) helpful.
   A. Well, I've heard that he's very aggressive (and / but) nice.

VOCABULARY   Student Course Book pp. 16–17

I. Circle the most appropriate adjective.

1. Designing roads and bridges is an | a. excited | job.
   | b. exciting |

2. The | a. confused | meteorologist gave the wrong forecast.
   | b. confusing |

3. The ambulance driver was | a. tired | after a busy night at the hospital.
   | b. tiring |

4. Living among people of other countries is a | a. fascinated | experience.
   | b. fascinating |

5. The new supervisor was not | a. amused | by the practical joke which
   | b. amusing |

   one of the employees played on him.

(continued)

6. Criminal law is an | a. interested | b. interesting | aspect of the legal system.

7. The monthly sales of the real estate agent were | a. disappointed | b. disappointing |

8. Graphic design is a | a. challenged | b. challenging | new field in the area of computers.

9. The congressman was | a. surprised | b. surprising | at the ability of his young speech writer.

10. A forest ranger's work, although quiet, is never | a. bored | b. boring |

II. Circle the best answer.

1. An _____ assistant handles business communication for an executive of a company.
    a. administration
    b. administrative
    c. administrator

2. An emergency medical _____ assists people with medical emergencies.
    a. technical
    b. technician
    c. technology

3. An _____ studies people from different cultures.
    a. anthropology
    b. anthropologist
    c. anthropologer

4. A fashion _____ creates new styles of clothing.
    a. design
    b. designist
    c. designer

5. A stock market _____ predicts economic changes.
    a. analyst
    b. analyze
    c. analyzist

When you meet people for the first time at social gatherings, there are certain questions you can safely ask them. In the United States, for example, questions about the kind of work you do, your place of work, and your position at work are perfectly acceptable. In some countries, however, they are considered inappropriate. Questions about your hobbies, where you live, and what kind of house you live in are also conversation starters in the United States. But in other parts of the world, they are thought to be too personal, as are questions about a person's religious, political, or ethical beliefs. While these are not the first questions you should ask an American, they would not be considered impolite after you've spoken to someone for a while. Some taboo topics of discussion in many countries include asking how much people earn, how old they are, and how much they have paid for particular items. Generally safe subjects are those that deal with generalities such as the weather or current events.

I. Underline the correct word.

1. You should (always/never) ask about a person's salary.

2. In the United States, people often talk about (religion/work) when they meet someone new.

3. "Taboo" means (safe/forbidden).

4. In the United States, people (rarely/usually) ask about a person's position in a company.

5. Questions about (age/the weather) are generally safe topics.

II. Check *Yes* or *No* according to the appropriateness of each of the following questions when first meeting someone.

			Yes	No
1.	"How do you like this weather?"	1.	✓	
2.	"Where do you work?"	2.	___	___
3.	"How much did you pay for your shoes?"	3.	___	___
4.	"Do you live around here?"	4.	___	___
5.	"What religion are you?"	5.	___	___
6.	"Do you enjoy your work?"	6.	___	___
7.	"Do you live in a house or an apartment?"	7.	___	___
8.	"How old are you?"	8.	___	___
9.	"What do you think about the speech the President made?"	9.	___	___
10.	"How much did your new car cost?"	10.	___	___

I. Complete the missing lines in the following conversation with appropriate questions or responses.

A student and a professor meet at a college orientation.

Professor: *Are you a student here?* _____

Student: Yes, I am. _____

Professor: Yes. I teach political science.

Student: _____

Professor: Yes, I do. Teaching young people is very challenging.

Student: _____

Professor: We discuss different systems of government and their effects on society. _____

_____

Student: Business Administration.

Professor: _____

Student: Yes, very much.

Professor: Well, I have to get to a class. _____

Student: It was nice meeting you, too.

II. Write a conversation between a man and a woman who have just met at a party.

Man: _____

Woman: _____

Man: _____

Woman: _____

Man: _____

Woman: _____

Man: _____

Woman: _____

Man: _____

Woman: _____

3

FUNCTIONS Student Course Book p. 20

Walter is going on a business trip to Dallas. He's asking his wife for suggestions about what he should pack for the trip. Write his wife's suggestions using the descriptive words below.

1. A. Which suit do you think I should take?

   B. _____

   (blue/white stripes)

2. A. I'll also need another suit. Which one do you think I should take?

   B. _____

   (dark brown/your mother gave you for your birthday)

3. A. Great idea! I'll also need a few ties. Which ones should I pack?

   B. _____

   (red/white dots) (brown/you bought in Italy)

4. A. What about a camera?

   B. _____

   (automatic/black leather case)

   A. Good idea! Thanks for your help. I couldn't have packed without you!

📼 **LISTENING** Student Course Book p. 20

Listen and decide where the conversation took place. Circle the best answer.

Example You will hear: A. Hello. I'm looking for a warm sweater.
                          B. How about this blue one made in Scotland?

             Answer: a. at someone's home
                      b. in Scotland
                      ©. in a department store

1. a. in an office
   b. in someone's home
   c. in a department store

2. a. at a formal party
   b. at someone's home
   c. at a department store

(continued)

3. a. in a supermarket
    b. in a camera shop
    c. in a leather shop

4. a. in a restaurant
    b. at the beach
    c. at the United Nations

5. a. in a French department store
    b. at a party
    c. at someone's home

6. a. at Aunt Helen's house
    b. in a restaurant
    c. at someone's home

🔲 **LISTENING**

Circle the answer that is *closest in meaning* to the sentence you hear.

Example   You will hear: Have you by any chance ever been to Taiwan?

Answer: a. Do you have a chance to go to Taiwan?
           (b.) Have you been to Taiwan before?
           c. You won the chance to go to Taiwan?

1. a. Can you tell me where New York City is?
    b. Can you tell me why you like New York City?
    c. Can you give me a description of New York City?

2. a. I know many exciting places, but this is more exciting than most.
    b. I don't know most of the exciting places.
    c. You know most of the exciting places.

3. a. Did you tell me anything else?
    b. What can you tell me?
    c. Do you know anything else?

4. a. Would you like to know Elsa?
    b. What other information interests you?
    c. Do you know anything else?

5. a. How are the people at the beaches feeling?
    b. What are the beaches and the people like?
    c. What do the people do at the beaches?

6. a. I'm sure you'll have a great time.
    b. I'm concerned it won't be far enough away.
    c. I'm worried you won't have a good time there.

7. a. I think your china is beautiful.
    b. I believe China is a very pretty country.
    c. I think you should visit China.

8. a. There's something the matter with you.
    b. I think you're correct.
    c. I don't believe you're right.

9. a. He asked me if the people were very friendly.
    b. You asked me if the people were very friendly.
    c. I think the people are very friendly.

10. a. The sound is wonderful in that place.
    b. I like the wonderful sound.
    c. It must be a wonderful place.

Write an appropriate response using the superlative form of the underlined adjective.

1. Don't you think Ellen is a <u>wonderful</u> person?

   <u>Yes, she's one of the most wonderful people I know.</u>

2. Isn't Uncle Harry <u>friendly</u>?

   _____

3. Don't you think this discotheque is <u>lively</u>?

   _____

4. Isn't this restaurant <u>nice</u>?

   _____

5. Isn't that little boy <u>intelligent</u>?

   _____

WRITING   Student Course Book p. 21

You've been hired by a travel magazine to write a short description of your country in order to attract tourists. First, make a list of five major tourist attractions and describe them using appropriate adjectives and their superlatives.

Tourist Attractions	Adjectives	Superlatives

Example

Eiffel Tower	tall	the tallest
1.		
2.		
3.		
4.		
5.		

Now write your description, trying to be as "convincing" as possible to the tourists you hope will visit your country.

Circle the best answer.

1. Did you tell the taxi driver _____?
   a. where do you want to go
   b. where you wanted to go
   c. where did you want to go

2. Do you remember _____?
   a. what time begins the performance
   b. what time does the performance begin
   c. what time the performance begins

3. Will you ask Mr. Talbot _____?
   a. when should I meet him
   b. when I should meet him
   c. when meet him should I

4. Can you tell me _____?
   a. why you're in a bad mood
   b. why are you in a bad mood
   c. why you in a bad mood

5. Do you understand _____?
   a. how works the machine
   b. how does the machine work
   c. how the machine works

6. Do you know anyone _____?
   a. who fixes bicycles
   b. who does fix bicycles
   c. who fix bicycles

7. Have you asked the boss _____?
   a. when is she going on her business trip
   b. when she going on her business trip
   c. when she is going on her business trip

8. Does your father by any chance know _____?
   a. who is the owner of the store
   b. who the owner is of the store
   c. who the owner of the store is

9. Did you happen to hear _____?
   a. what the teacher said
   b. what did the teacher say
   c. what said the teacher

10. Do you ever wonder _____?
    a. when things will change
    b. when will things change
    c. when do things change

Read each direct quote. Then circle the statement that best reports about that quote. Remember to check for the sequence of tenses.

1. "This movie is terrible."
   a. I thought that movie is terrible.
   b. I thought that movie was terrible.
   c. I thought that is a terrible movie.

2. "Were you at the lecture last night?"
   a. Professor Jones asked was I at the lecture last night.
   b. Professor Jones asked if I had been at the lecture last night.
   c. Professor Jones asked that I was at the lecture last night.

3. "I'm not going to the dance with you!"
   a. He exclaimed that he wasn't going to the dance with me.
   b. He exclaimed that he will not go to the dance with me.
   c. He exclaimed that he had not gone to the dance with me.

4. "Everything will be all right."
   a. The police assured me that everything will be all right.
   b. The police assured me that everything had been all right.
   c. The police assured me that everything would be all right.

5. "Can I pay you next week?"
   a. She wondered whether can she pay me next week.
   b. She wondered whether could she pay me next week.
   c. She wondered whether she could pay me next week.

6. "I didn't finish my homework."
   a. Tom admitted that he didn't finished his homework.
   b. Tom admitted that he hadn't finished his homework.
   c. Tom admitted that he didn't finish his homework.

7. "The store does not open until 10:00 A.M."
   a. He emphasized that the store does not open until 10:00 A.M.
   b. He emphasized that the store won't open until 10:00 A.M.
   c. He emphasized that the store did not open until 10:00 A.M.

8. "I have a lot to do tonight."
   a. He said he has a lot to do tonight.
   b. He said he had a lot to do tonight.
   c. He said if he had a lot to do tonight.

9. "Were you telling the truth?"
   a. The lawyer asked the criminal if he had been telling the truth.
   b. The lawyer asked the criminal if he was telling the truth.
   c. The lawyer asked the criminal had he been telling the truth.

10. "Would you please go to the bank for me?"
    a. He asked me if would I go to the bank for him.
    b. He asked me if I will go to the bank for him.
    c. He asked me if I would go to the bank for him.

Before Johann Guttenburg developed the printing press in 1437, news traveled by word of mouth. This meant that information was slow to reach the public and that details changed as news spread from one person to the next. Printed matter, such as newspapers, made it possible for information to be gathered in a central office and for news items to be written more accurately. In 1844 Samuel Morse perfected a system of sending coded messages through electrical wires, establishing an early form of long-distance communication. The network of communications expanded in 1858 through the work of Julius von Reuter, who extended the reach of newspapers by telegraphing news bulletins to different countries. With each of these developments, the public marveled at the ingenuity of the communications pioneers and asked, "What will they think of next?"

"They" thought of plenty. Alexander Graham Bell conceived of the idea of transmitting speech by electrical impulses and perfected the first telephone in 1876. The invention of the "wireless" by Guglielmo Marconi in 1895 paved the way for modern-day radio transmission. V. K. Zworykin worked on one of the first televisions in 1928 using an electronic scanning device.

Communications reached new heights when televisions were mass produced in the 1950s. The 1962 launching of Telstar, the first communications satellite, enabled people to witness live events broadcast from anywhere in the world. Underground and underwater cables also transmitted programs from one area to another, increasing the efficiency of information dissemination. Telecommunications and computer networking are testimonies to the enormous technological advances of our times and hint at even greater developments to come.

I. Write *True* or *False.*

1. The printing press was perfected in the fourteenth century.   _____

2. Samuel Morse worked on a form of long-distance communication we now call the telegraph.   _____

3. Alexander Graham Bell gave the first speech on the radio in 1895.   _____

4. Televisions were manufactured in large numbers during the decade of the 1950s.   _____

5. Satellites do not transmit live television programs.   _____

II. Circle the best answer.

1. Although many other means of communication have been _____, a great number of people still read newspapers.
    a. perfect   b. perfected   c. perfection

2. After Sputnik I was launched in 1957, the U.S. government realized the necessity of _____ space research.
    a. expanding   b. expand   c. expansion

3. Two companies that _____ satellites in the United States are RCA and the Hughes Aircraft Company.
    a. production   b. producing   c. produce

4. The _____ of programs by cable enables viewers to watch movies, sports, or news twenty-four hours a day.
   a. transmits   b. transmission   c. transmit

5. The _____ of computer technology has been aided by the microchip.
   a. develop   b. developing   c. development

6. Now a person can _____ bank, shop, pay bills, and reserve tickets using a television set and keyboard at home thanks to a system called Videotex.
   a. conceivably   b. conception   c. conceive

7. Computer "whiz kids" are _____ to the fact that early introduction to the computer facilitates learning.
   a. testimonies   b. testify   c. tests

8. If communications pioneers of the past were alive today, they would probably be contributing to the _____ advances of the present.
   a. marvelously   b. marvel   c. marvelous

WRITING

Student Course Book p. 24

List the five most common ways that you get information in your daily life. Then list five ways your grandparents probably received information.

	Present	Past
1.	_____	_____
2.	_____	_____
3.	_____	_____
4.	_____	_____
5.	_____	_____

Write a paragraph comparing modern communications with those of your grandparents' time.

Listen and circle the appropriate tag question.

Example   You will hear: Arthur was fired, _____?

                    Answer: ⓐ wasn't he?
                                b. did he?

1. a. won't they?   5. a. did you?
    b. didn't they?   b. didn't you?

2. a. did it?   6. a. aren't you?
    b. isn't it?   b. haven't you?

3. a. will you?   7. a. are you?
    b. won't you?   b. aren't you?

4. a. did you?   8. a. aren't you?
    b. have you?   b. will you?

GRAMMAR CHECK: *Tag Questions*   Student Course Book p. 24

Write an appropriate tag question for the following statements.

1. He can't go, _____?

2. You aren't Peter Smith, _____?

3. You'll take care of it, _____?

4. Sally's not going to go to work today, _____?

5. You took the package to the post office, _____?

6. You're kidding, _____?

7. Shirley's been there before, _____?

8. We haven't gone very far, _____?

9. You won't be late, _____?

10. They can do that, _____?

11. We didn't have an assignment in history class last night, _____?

12. The office is going to be closed tomorrow, _____?

Listen and decide according to the intonation whether or not the speaker is surprised.

Example   You will hear: They're going to build a
                                 school across the street?!

                   Answer: ⓐ surprised
                              b. not surprised

                              She's just been promoted.

                              a. surprised
                              ⓑ not surprised

1. a. surprised   6. a. surprised
    b. not surprised   b. not surprised

2. a. surprised   7. a. surprised
    b. not surprised   b. not surprised

3. a. surprised   8. a. surprised
    b. not surprised   b. not surprised

4. a. surprised   9. a. surprised
    b. not surprised   b. not surprised

5. a. surprised   10. a. surprised
    b. not surprised   b. not surprised

FUNCTIONS

For each of the following dialogs, circle the appropriate line for Speaker B.

1. A. John's getting married!
    B. a. You've got to believe it!
        b. That can't be it!
        c. You've got to be kidding!

2. A. Do you think Nancy will really move?
    B. a. I'm not completely kidding.
        b. I'm not a hundred percent.
        c. I don't know for sure.

3. A. The President is resigning!
    B. a. No believing!
        b. Oh, come on!
        c. Where can you hear that?

4. A. Do you think it's true?
    B. a. I'm absolutely positive.
        b. I can't know for sure.
        c. I'm completely kidding.

5. A. Alice is going out with Karl!
    B. a. Where did you know that?
        b. I don't believe it!
        c. I'm a hundred percent.

6. A. They're making the parking lot into a
            park!
    B. a. How do you know that?
        b. I don't know.
        c. I'm positively.

7. A. The neighbors are building
            a tennis court!
    B. a. Are you completely sure?
        b. Who told you that?
        c. That can't be positive!

8. A. There's going to be a hurricane tonight!
    B. a. Don't you know for sure?
        b. Are you positively?
        c. That can't be!

I. For each of the following dialogs, circle the most appropriate line for Speaker B.

1. A. I'm going to Alaska!
    B. a. How are you doing?
        b. What do you want to know?
        c. That's fantastic!

2. A. His company went out of business last year.
    B. a. I'm absolutely positive.
        b. What a shame!
        c. How do you do?

3. A. I'm going to a job interview and I don't know what to wear.
    B. a. I'm very sorry to hear that.
        b. Have you heard anything else?
        c. How about your blue suit?

4. A. The weather is very pleasant in Georgia, and in my opinion, the people there are very nice.
    B. a. What else can you tell me?
        b. How about you?
        c. How are things?

5. A. Word has it that Larry has a new girlfriend.
    B. a. I forgot all about it.
        b. I'm very happy for you.
        c. You're kidding!

6. A. Tell me a little about yourself.
    B. a. What else have you heard?
        b. What would you like to know?
        c. I'm absolutely positive.

7. A. I haven't seen you in so long. How have you been?
    B. a. I'm glad to meet you.
        b. Excuse me.
        c. Not bad.

8. A. You didn't by any chance remember to turn on the dryer, did you?
    B. a. I'm sure.
        b. Which one is that?
        c. Oh, it completely slipped my mind.

9. A. Everybody says she's wonderful.
    B. a. Really? That's interesting.
        b. What a pity!
        c. What do you do?

10. A. Somehow I thought he was going to arrive later than you.
     B. a. Okay.
         b. I don't think so.
         c. I forgot all about it.

II. For each of the following dialogs, circle the most appropriate line for Speaker A.

1. A. a. Nice to meet you.
        b. I was going for a walk, when suddenly I heard a scream.
        c. I'm going to Florida next week.
    B. So what did you do?

2. A. a. How far did you travel?
        b. Did anybody call me?
        c. Do you know where the supermarket is?
    B. Not as far as I know.

3. A. a. How about you?
        b. Are you leaving soon?
        c. Did your mother have anything to say?
    B. Not really. We just talked for a few seconds.

4. A. a. I don't think we've met.
        b. How are you?
        c. Guess who I saw yesterday!
    B. I'm Sam.

III. Circle the best answer.

1. _____ by any chance know where
    the bus stop is?
    a. Do you
    b. Have you
    c. Will you

2. _____ tell me anything else?
    a. Will
    b. Don't you
    c. Can you

3. Can you tell me _____?
    a. what it's like
    b. what did you do next
    c. where did you hear that

4. Let me _____ to my cousin, Jim.
    a. meet you
    b. tell you something more
    c. introduce you

5. He's _____ with the blond hair.
    a. the one
    b. who
    c. the boy who

6. I'm very happy _____ that.
    a. do you know
    b. as far as I know
    c. to hear

4

Listen and circle the best answer.

Example   You will hear: A.   Excuse me, but would you mind turning down your radio? I'm trying to study.
                                    B.   I'm sorry. I didn't hear you. What did you say?

                   Answer: a.   He asked her to study with him.
                               b.   He asked her to turn on the radio.
                               ©   He couldn't study because her radio was disturbing him.

1.   a.   He asked her to get thirty-two books.
    b.   He asked her to repeat what she had read in the book.
    c.   He told her what page to look at, but she didn't hear him.

2.   a.   He offered to carry her bags.
    b.   He didn't want to carry her bags.
    c.   He told her to carry her bags.

3.   a.   He missed ice cream sodas.
    b.   He suggested ordering an ice cream soda.
    c.   He thought the ice cream sundaes were delicious.

4.   a.   He didn't like the station on the TV.
    b.   He was going to the station.
    c.   He asked her to take the TV to the station.

5.   a.   She gave him a wrench.
    b.   She was tired.
    c.   She gave him her hand.

6.   a.   He asked her to turn off the stereo and go to sleep.
    b.   He asked her to turn on the stereo.
    c.   He asked her to turn down the stereo.

7.   a.   He was trying to give her directions, but she didn't hear him.
    b.   He was trying to catch a bus.
    c.   He wanted to know if he was right.

8.   a.   She didn't hear him because she wasn't near him.
    b.   She didn't hear him because she was copying the report.
    c.   She didn't hear him ask her to copy the report.

9.   a.   He asked her to get the flies off the hamburger.
    b.   He asked her to fry his hamburger, but she didn't hear him.
    c.   He wanted french fries and a hamburger.

Circle the correct question word.

1. Please be here by 6:00 A.M.

   | a. Where |
   | b. When | do you want me to be here?
   | c. How |

2. Give these packages to the people in Apartment 2C.

   | a. Who |
   | b. Where | do you want me to give these to?
   | c. What |

3. Get two loaves of bread and some butter at the supermarket, okay?

   | a. Where |
   | b. What | do you want me to get?
   | c. How |

4. Take these vitamins twice a day.

   | a. What |
   | b. How often | do you want me to take them?
   | c. How |

5. Put three coins in the machine.

   | a. How much |
   | b. How | coins should I put in?
   | c. How many |

6. Tom and I are leaving for the opera at 7:00 P.M.

   | a. When |
   | b. Who | are you going at 7:00 P.M.?
   | c. Why |

7. I'm leaving for Mexico on the 9:00 A.M. plane.

   | a. How often |
   | b. Where | are you leaving for Mexico?
   | c. When |

8. The math course ends on December 15th.

   | a. When |
   | b. Which | course ends then?
   | c. Why |

9. My father runs three times a week.

   | a. What |
   | b. How often | does he run?
   | c. Who |

10. Allen is getting married to Lisa next month.

    | a. When |
    | b. How often | is he getting married to?
    | c. Who |

Listen and follow the directions to different places on the map. Decide where you are on the map and circle the best answer. Each set of directions will *always begin from point X* on your map.

Example   You will hear: A. Can you tell me how to get to the bank?
                              B. Sure. Walk two blocks down Main Street and turn left. The bank is on the left.

                              Where is the bank?

              Answer: ⓐ. A
                        b. B
                        c. C

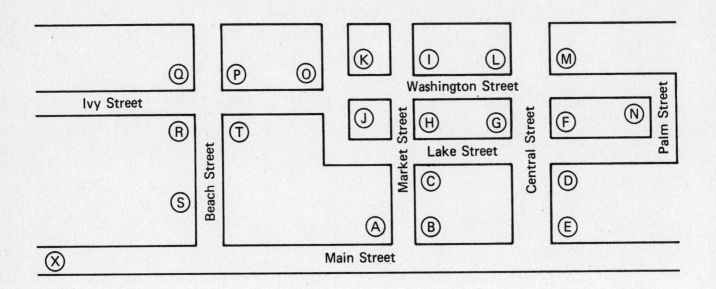

1.	a.	D
	b.	F
	c.	M
2.	a.	R
	b.	T
	c.	P
3.	a.	G
	b.	M
	c.	L

4.	a.	O
	b.	J
	c.	K
5.	a.	P
	b.	R
	c.	Q
6.	a.	M
	b.	N
	c.	F

Circle the word that does not relate to the rest of the words in the group.

1. a. block   b. street   c. road   d. traffic

2. a. jack   b. lift   c. rest   d. raise

3. a. tight   b. secure   c. fixed   d. strong

4. a. fruit   b. nuts   c. bolts   d. screws

5. a. take off   b. take out   c. release   d. remove

6. a. unscrew   b. loosen   c. untwist   d. tighten

7. a. pump   b. explode   c. fill   d. inflate

8. a. tire   b. flat   c. deflated   d. empty

9. a. nozzle   b. spout   c. gas   d. faucet

10. a. tank   b. army   c. receptacle   d. compartment

GRAMMAR CHECK: *Two-Word Verbs*   Student Course Book pp. 34–35

Choose the appropriate preposition from the list below to best complete the meaning of the sentences.

for	**on**	**off**
up	**around**	**in**

1. Kate has been waiting _____ her brother for over an hour. She's angry because he's late.

2. You're going the wrong way. Turn _____ on this street and take a right at the first stop sign.

3. First, you pick _____ the receiver and then you insert a quarter.

4. Take _____ the old sticker and put _____ the new one.

5. The auto mechanic raised the car _____ with a jack in order to change the tires.

6. To get a pack of gum from this machine, put _____ fifty cents and pull the lever.

There are many stereotypes about the character of people in various parts of the United States. In the Northeast and Midwest, people are said to be closed and private. In the South and West, however, they are often thought of as being more open and hospitable. Ask someone from St. Louis where the nearest sandwich shop is, and he or she will politely give you directions. A New Yorker might eye you suspiciously at first and after deciding it is safe to talk to you, might give you a rather abrupt explanation. A person from Georgia might be very gracious about directing you and even suggest some alternative places to eat. A Texan just might take you to the place and treat you to lunch!

American stereotypes are abundant. New Englanders are often thought of as being friendly and helpful, but reserved. Southerners are known for their hospitality and warmth. People from the western part of the United States are often considered very outgoing. These variations in character can be traced to different factors such as climate, living conditions, and historical development.

When traveling from region to region, Americans themselves are often surprised at the differing degrees of friendliness in the United States.

I. Write *True* or *False.*

1. Americans make generalizations about how people from certain
    areas behave.   _____

2. New Yorkers are usually open with strangers.   _____

3. People from the South are considered gracious hosts.   _____

4. Weather has an effect on regional character.   _____

5. The friendliest Americans travel from region to region.   _____

II. Circle the word closest in meaning to the underlined word.

1. Stereotypes about people are not necessarily true.
    a. fixed ideas   b. descriptions   c. conclusions

2. She made few friends because of her closed manner.
    a. suspicious   b. gracious   c. private

3. The owners of that country inn are extremely hospitable.
    a. healthy   b. gracious   c. sickly

4. The police officer eyed the suspect suspiciously.
    a. winked at   b. ignored   c. observed

5. His abrupt departure left everyone uneasy.
    a. broken   b. hasty   c. abnormal

6. The main road is under construction; we have to take an alternative route.
    a. a shorter   b. a longer   c. another

7. On Sundays our family would walk in the park and Dad would <u>treat us</u> to ice cream.
   a. taste   b. buy   c. talk about

8. Our neighbor's vegetable harvest was so <u>abundant</u> that she gave us several baskets of tomatoes and beans.
   a. adequate   b. scarce   c. plentiful

9. Because she had been sickly all her life, the child was not very <u>outgoing</u>.
   a. sociable   b. well   c. athletic

10. The historian <u>traced</u> our family tree back five generations.
    a. drew   b. followed the   c. looked for
                             development of

WRITING Student Course Book pp. 34–35

Make a list of all the descriptive words found in the reading. Add other words that describe people's characteristics and personalities.

closed, polite, warm

_____

_____

Now make a list of different regions of your country and the words that best describe the characteristics and personalities of people who live there.

Region	Descriptive Words

Are these true characteristics or merely stereotypes? What factors influence our perceptions of people in other places? Write a paragraph to explain.

Listen and circle the best response to Speaker A.

Example   You will hear: Could you possibly tell me where Main Street is?

               Answer: a.   Yes, that's right.
                              b.   Do you follow me?
                             ©   Sure.

1. a. I haven't.
    b. I think you understand.
    c. I think so.

2. a. I follow you.
    b. Uh-húh.
    c. Thank you.

3. a. Then what do I do?
    b. I forget.
    c. Do you follow me?

4. a. Let me understand.
    b. It's possibly.
    c. Sure.

5. a. Yes, it's far.
    b. Yes, I'm mixed up.
    c. Yes, I see.

6. a. No. I'm not okay.
    b. No. I'm following you.
    c. No. I'm lost.

7. a. No, I haven't.
    b. No. I'm afraid I didn't get that.
    c. No. I'm not understanding.

8. a. Yes. I'm lost.
    b. Okay. I've got it.
    c. No. I lost the instructions.

FUNCTIONS

Circle the best answer.

1. _____ know how to get to the bank?
    a. Could you by any chance
    b. Would you be able
    c. Do you by any chance

2. Walk three blocks, turn left, and then go right. _____?
    a. Have you follow me?
    b. Let me understand?
    c. Okay?

3. _____ where the post office is?
    a. Do you possible know
    b. Could you possibly tell me
    c. Would you chance know

4. _____ show me how to change this tire?
    a. Would possible
    b. Do you know
    c. Could you

5. First take Route 1, then take Exit 5. _____?
    a. Have you got it?
    b. Have you get it?
    c. Did you have it?

6. I'm lost. _____ how to find School Street?
   a. Can you tell me
   b. Would you possibly by any chance
   c. Can you please

7. Pick up the nozzle, put it in the tank, and press the handle to start. _____?
   a. Yes?
   b. Let me see?
   c. Do you follow me?

8. Mix together four eggs, salt, pepper, and milk. _____?
   a. Now are you lost?
   b. Are you with me so far?
   c. Didn't you see?

9. Could you repeat _____?
   a. where are you
   b. the direction things you said
   c. the last two instructions

10. I'm not _____ you.
    a. lost
    b. following
    c. get

▭▭ LISTENING   Student Course Book pp. 36–37

Listen carefully to the instructions and decide what process is being described. Circle the best answer.

Example   You will hear: First, put in one teaspoon of coffee.
                                 Then, add boiling water and stir.

                    Answer: a. mixing a drink
                              (b.) making a cup of coffee
                               c. making a cup of tea

1. a. buying a can of soda
   b. making a deposit
   c. buying candy

2. a. taping together a piece of paper
   b. starting a tape recorder
   c. turning off a tape recorder

3. a. giving directions to a store
   b. writing a check
   c. making a calendar

4. a. locking up a car
   b. igniting a fire
   c. starting a car with an alarm

5. a. sewing a button
   b. taking a picture
   c. taking an eye exam

6. a. turning on a light
   b. making a lamp
   c. changing a light bulb

5

Listen and decide where the conversation took place. Circle the best answer.

Example   You will hear: A. That was some performance!
                              B. Thanks.

                   Answer: ⓐ at a play
                              b. at a gas station
                              c. at a playground

1. a. at a supermarket
    b. at a restaurant
    c. at a bakery

2. a. in a fresh-vegetable store
    b. at a photography exhibit
    c. at a university

3. a. in a drug store
    b. at a department store
    c. at an advertising agency

4. a. in an office
    b. in a library
    c. at a tennis court

5. a. at someone's home
    b. at City Hall
    c. at a movie theater

6. a. at a music store
    b. at the symphony
    c. at a pastry shop

7. a. on a farm
    b. in a supermarket
    c. at a school

8. a. in a camera store
    b. in an art class
    c. at a bank

Listen and decide what the relationship between the two speakers is. Circle the best answer.

Example   You will hear: A. Emily is a wonderful student.
                              B. Oh, I'm so glad to hear that.

                   Answer: ⓐ teacher–parent
                              b. brother–sister
                              c. actor–director

1. a. banker–customer
    b. doctor–patient
    c. accountant–client

2. a. mechanic–customer
    b. husband–wife
    c. teacher–student

3. a. professor–student
   b. employer–employee
   c. employee–employer

4. a. ticket taker–moviegoer
   b. librarian–student
   c. police officer–driver

5. a. father–child
   b. waiter–customer
   c. pianist–audience member

6. a. student–student
   b. lawyer–criminal
   c. nurse–doctor

7. a. mother–child
   b. homeowner–gardener
   c. customer–laundry owner

8. a. real estate agent–client
   b. politician–supporter
   c. shop owner–customer

FUNCTIONS Student Course Book p. 41

For each of the following dialogs, circle the most appropriate line for Speaker B.

1. A. I really like your necklace. It's very attractive.
   B. a. I'm not really serious.
      b. I'm being nice to you.
      c. Oh, go on!

2. A. That suit is one of the nicest suits I've ever seen.
   B. a. Thanks for being honest.
      b. Oh, come on! You're just saying that.
      c. I'm really honest.

3. A. Your new hairstyle is really wonderful.
   B. a. Absolutely.
      b. Fabulous.
      c. Thanks.

4. A. Oh, go on! You're just saying that.
   B. a. No. I mean it.
      b. No, thanks.
      c. Well, I'm glad.

5. A. I really love your glasses. They're so stylish.
   B. a. I've never seen them.
      b. It's nice of you for saying so.
      c. You're just saying that!

6. A. You've written the most interesting and unusual poems.
   B. a. Well, it's nice.
      b. Well, thanks for saying so.
      c. Well, I'm glad you're going on.

7. A. Did you really like the speech I gave?
   B. a. It's the most fabulous.
      b. Absolutely.
      c. I'm really glad.

8. A. This chocolate cake you made is delicious!
   B. a. That was quite nice.
      b. Well, thanks for meaning it.
      c. It's nice of you to say that.

9. A. You look great! You've lost so much weight!
   B. a. Aw, go on!
      b. Be really serious!
      c. I'm honest.

10. A. I really love your office. It's so beautifully designed!
    B. a. Oh, go!
       b. Oh, come on!
       c. Oh, well.

Everyone needs a "pat on the back" now and then, but compliments are often easier to give than to receive, especially for Americans. Tell an American that he or she plays a great game of tennis, and the compliment will probably be shrugged off with "It must be my lucky day" or "This new racket is wonderful" or "My tennis teacher is fantastic." Of course, a person might also smile and say "Thank you," but many Americans downplay compliments by giving the credit to someone or something else.

It is interesting to compare how people from different cultures react to compliments. In some countries, if you compliment someone on a possession, he or she will give it to you or tell you that you may use it whenever you like. In other countries, a person will make a derogatory remark about it to show humility and unworthiness of praise. However, in most cultures compliments are received with gratitude.

A current form of complimenting is referred to as "stroking," the praise or positive feedback people give each other, especially at the workplace. American companies understand the importance of giving recognition to employees in order to maintain morale and assure worker performance. Companies often give rewards for outstanding achievement and service.

I. Match the words in the first column with their meanings in the second column.

a.	achievement	1.	_____	lessen
b.	current	2.	_____	pass, not accept
c.	derogatory	3.	_____	acknowledge
d.	downplay	4.	_____	negative
e.	feedback	5.	_____	modesty
f.	give credit	6.	_____	response
g.	humility	7.	_____	spirit
h.	morale	8.	_____	being without value
i.	shrug off	9.	_____	present-day
j.	unworthiness	10.	_____	successful effort

II. Circle the best answer.

1. In the first paragraph, "pat on the back" means
   a. a compliment.
   b. a caress.
   c. a hit.

2. How do Americans downplay compliments?
   a. They pat each other on the back.
   b. They smile and say "Thank you."
   c. They say that someone or something else is responsible.

3. In the second paragraph, "a derogatory remark" is made by
   a. the person giving the compliment.
   b. the person receiving the compliment.
   c. both of them.

4. According to the reading, how do people of some cultures react to compliments?
   a. They compare them.
   b. They give or let you use their possessions.
   c. They praise themselves.

5. In the third paragraph, "stroking" means
   a. praising.
   b. feeding.
   c. referring.

6. How do some companies give compliments?
   a. They feedback their employees.
   b. They make their employees perform.
   c. They give their employees rewards.

WRITING

Student Course Book p. 41

---

1. You are an executive in a large company. Write a note to an employee to compliment him or her for excellent performance. (Be specific about the qualities and achievements that you are complimenting.)

2. You are a loyal fan of a famous performer. You have just seen this performer's most recent movie, play, television show, or concert. Write a note to compliment him or her for this performance, and tell why you admire this person so much. (Be specific about the qualities of the performance you found exceptional.)

3. You are an English teacher, and it's the end of the term. Write a note to your best student to compliment him or her for being outstanding. (Be specific about your student's particular achievements during the term.)

Circle the best answer for the following situations.

1. Ted is six feet three inches tall. There's a bed he wants to buy, but it's only six feet long.
    a. The bed is too long.
    b. The bed isn't long enough.

2. Sara has a twenty-eight-inch waist. There's a skirt she wants to buy, but it only has a twenty-four-inch waist.
    a. The skirt is too tight.
    b. The skirt isn't tight enough.

3. Ed is going to a formal party, and he needs to buy a new suit to wear to the party.
    a. His old suit is too formal.
    b. His old suit isn't formal enough.

4. Diane wears size 6 shoes; however, there's a pair of size 8 shoes she likes very much.
    a. The shoes are too big.
    b. The shoes are big enough.

5. John wants to wear a bulky winter sweater underneath his jacket. Unfortunately, his jacket is a little tight on him.
    a. The sweater is too bulky.
    b. The sweater is bulky enough.

6. Marcia needs a new mattress because she has a bad back. Her friend offered her a mattress, but it didn't help her back very much.
    a. The mattress was soft enough.
    b. The mattress was too soft.

7. The nutrition experiment requires a person who weighs less than 115 pounds. Alex weighs 140 pounds.
    a. Alex is heavy enough.
    b. Alex is too heavy.

8. Jennifer has to wrap a large gift, but she has only a very small box.
    a. The box isn't too large.
    b. The box isn't large enough.

9. Jane wants to wear her new winter coat outside, but it's seventy degrees.
    a. The coat is warm enough.
    b. The coat is too warm.

10. The teacher wanted to challenge her students, but she gave them a very easy assignment.
    a. The assignment was easy enough.
    b. The assignment was too easy.

Circle the best answer.

1. _____ did you like the book you just finished?
   a. When
   b. What
   c. How

2. What do you _____ my new computer?
   a. have in mind
   b. think of
   c. want

3. It _____ too expensive, is it?
   a. isn't
   b. wasn't
   c. wouldn't be

4. It's just _____.
   a. what I looked for
   b. what I minded
   c. what I had in mind

5. So you're _____ with it?
   a. pleasing
   b. satisfying
   c. satisfied

6. Yes, it's _____.
   a. very much
   b. perfect
   c. very

7. I wouldn't want it _____ lighter.
   a. any
   b. very
   c. so

8. No, not _____.
   a. fine
   b. happy
   c. at all

9. Is it _____?
   a. just what I mind
   b. satisfied with it
   c. long enough

10. How do you _____ the new chair?
    a. sit
    b. think of
    c. like

▭ LISTENING

Listen and answer the question "What is the customer buying?"

1. a. a mattress
   b. a dress
   c. a typewriter

2. a. a blouse
   b. a book
   c. a tennis racquet

3. a. a ring
   b. a coat
   c. a chair

4. a. shoes
   b. umbrellas
   c. socks

5. a. a sweater
   b. fruit
   c. a stereo

6. a. a radio
   b. a dress
   c. a pair of glasses

7. a. a scale
   b. a tie
   c. a puzzle

8. a. earrings
   b. gloves
   c. belts

Circle the best answer.

1. Anne's directions were confusing. Bob's were

    | a. too simple |
    | b. much simpler |
    | c. any simpler |

    than hers.

2. Kenny has several tennis racquets. His ten-year-old son wanted to borrow one of the racquets, but all of

    them were

    | a. too big |
    | b. big enough |
    | c. bigger |

    for his small hand.

3. Bill wants to go out with Linda because she's

    | a. pretty enough |
    | b. the prettiest |
    | c. the prettier |

    in the class.

4. Steve hopes to join the basketball team, but he's afraid he isn't

    | a. short enough |
    | b. any taller |
    | c. tall enough |

    to play.

5. Marianne's sports car is bright red. It's the

    | a. flashier |
    | b. flashy |
    | c. flashiest |

    car I've ever seen.

6. My mother and father never agree on politics. My father is

    | a. too conservative as |
    | b. as conservative as |
    | c. more conservative than |

    my mother.

7. Sam is only five feet five inches tall. The rest of the people in his family are very tall. No one else in his

    family is

    | a. short enough as |
    | b. shorter than |
    | c. the shortest as |

    he is.

8. Those children never stop talking! They're certainly

    | a. the most talkative |
    | b. more talkative |
    | c. any more talkative |

    than any other children I

    know.

9. Roger studies all the time, but his sister doesn't. Roger is

    | a. more serious than |
    | b. too serious as |
    | c. as serious as |

    his sister.

10. Freddy's joke was very funny, but it wasn't

    | a. any funnier |
    | b. the funniest as |
    | c. as funny as |

    Harry's joke was.

Listen and circle the answer that is *closest in meaning* to the sentence you have heard.

Example   You will hear: The movie wasn't as good as I thought it would be.

Answer: a.   I didn't think the movie would be good.
(b.) I didn't like the movie very much.
c.   The movie will be good.

1. a.   You didn't tell me the truth about my grades.
b.   You were disappointed with my grades.
c.   My grades were disappointing.

2. a.   Honestly, it was terrible.
b.   You were terribly honest.
c.   I thought you were honest.

3. a.   I hoped the class wouldn't be any shorter.
b.   I hoped the class would be shorter.
c.   I hoped for a long class.

4. a.   I expected the waterfalls to be spectacular.
b.   The waterfalls were wonderful.
c.   I expected the waterfalls to be boring.

5. a.   I didn't think Helen was honest with you.
b.   Helen couldn't have been nicer.
c.   Helen was nice.

6. a.   Were you disappointed you came?
b.   Why were you pleased?
c.   Why were you disappointed?

7. a.   I thought Linda's presentation would be uninteresting.
b.   I didn't think about Linda's presentation.
c.   Linda was interested in my thoughts about her presentation.

8. a.   John's partner was challenged.
b.   John was challenged.
c.   John didn't expect his partner to be bad.

9. a.   Brian was dishonest.
b.   The company was not pleased with Brian's work.
c.   Brian was disappointed with the work the company did for him.

10. a.   The score of the game was disappointing.
b.   The baseball player wasn't playing in the game.
c.   The game wasn't being scored.

Circle the best answer.

1. Why do you always _____ to feed your fish?
   a. forget
   b. forgetting
   c. forgot

2. _____ to her about the new position?
   a. Has you spoken
   b. Have you speak
   c. Have you spoken

3. If _____ bothers you, tell him.
   a. him singing
   b. his singing
   c. he sang

4. Why _____ you mentioned it to Joe yet?
   a. do
   b. don't
   c. haven't

5. But I _____ like to complain.
   a. haven't
   b. don't
   c. have

6. My neighbors are always _____ me.
   a. upset with
   b. upsetting with
   c. upset

7. Their _____ the radio late at night angers me.
   a. play
   b. played
   c. playing

8. _____ always making silly mistakes.
   a. He's
   b. His
   c. He'd

9. I _____ understand why you say that.
   a. haven't
   b. have
   c. don't

10. His old girlfriend is constantly _____ him love letters.
    a. sends
    b. sending
    c. sent

Listen to the conversations and decide how Speaker B feels about Speaker A's suggestion.

Example You will hear: A. How about seeing a science fiction movie tonight?
B. Well, to tell you the truth, I don't like science fiction movies very much. How about a western?

Answer: a. likes the idea
(b.) dislikes the idea

1. a. likes the idea
    b. dislikes the idea

2. a. likes the idea
    b. dislikes the idea

3. a. likes the idea
    b. dislikes the idea

4. a. likes the idea
    b. dislikes the idea

5. a. likes the idea
    b. dislikes the idea

6. a. likes the idea
    b. dislikes the idea

7. a. likes the idea
    b. dislikes the idea

8. a. likes the idea
    b. dislikes the idea

9. a. likes the idea
    b. dislikes the idea

10. a. likes the idea
    b. dislikes the idea

Choose either A or B.

A. You are a restaurant reviewer for a gourmet food magazine. You have just been asked to write a review of a local restaurant. Your review can be either positive or negative.
   Make a list of the food you have tried at a particular restaurant. Describe the food, and give it a rating of 1–5 (5 is the highest rating; 1 is the lowest).

Restaurant	Food	Description	Rating

Now use this information to write your review.

B. You are an arts critic for your local newspaper. Write a positive or negative review of a movie you have seen recently. Include details about the acting, directing, photography, plot, and so on.

6

In 1955, a man named Raymond Kroc entered a partnership with two brothers named McDonald. They operated a popular restaurant in California which sold food that was easy to prepare and serve quickly. Hamburgers, french fries, and cold drinks were the main items on the limited menu. Kroc opened similar eating places under the same name, "McDonald's," and they were an instant success. He later took over the company, and today it is one of the most famous and successful "fast-food" chains in America and the world.

Why was his idea so successful? Probably the most significant reason was that his timing was right. In the 1950s, most married women stayed home to keep house and take care of their children. During the decade of the 1960s, the movement for equality between the sexes and an economy that required more families to have two wage-earners resulted in many women returning to the workplace. This meant that they had less time and energy to devote to housework and preparation of meals, so they relied more on "TV dinners" and fast-food restaurants.

Single parents also have little time to spend in the kitchen. Convenience foods, processed and packaged, help a great deal. People living alone because of divorce or a preference for a "singles lifestyle" also depend on this type of food, since cooking for one is often more trouble than it is worth. Food manufacturers have begun catering to this new market and now sell smaller portions specially prepared for just one person.

Fast food, or junk food as it is sometimes called, is not part of the diet of all Americans. Another trend of the 1960s, sometimes called the back-to-nature-movement or the hippie movement, influenced many people to avoid food that was packaged or processed. More and more Americans based their diets on natural foods containing no chemicals such as additives, preservatives, or artificial colors or flavors. This preference for natural foods continues to this day. These products can now be found not only in the special health food stores but also on the shelves of many supermarkets.

The success of Raymond Kroc's fast-food business and the increasing interest in natural foods are illustrations of the way in which social and economic trends influence where and what we eat.

Circle the correct answer.

1. "Cooking for one is more trouble than it is worth" means
   a. cooking for several people is worth more money.
   b. it takes too much time and effort to cook for one person.
   c. there are more problems when one person cooks.

2. In the third paragraph, "Food manufacturers have begun catering to this new market" means
   a. food companies are trying to serve single people.
   b. new supermarkets are being opened by food companies.
   c. catering services are being run by food companies.

3. "An economy that requires more than one wage earner" means
   a. one has to earn more wages in this economy.
   b. a wage earner requires more economics.
   c. more than one person in the family has to work in this economy.

4. "The two trends of the 1960s were single parents and the hippie movement" means
   a. many people raised children alone or were hippies.
   b. single parents tended to be hippies.
   c. 60 percent of the single parents and hippies moved.

5. "More and more Americans based their diets on natural foods" means
   a. Americans naturally had more food in their diets.
   b. Americans eliminated more natural food from their diets.
   c. Americans increasingly eliminated processed food from their diets.

6. The main idea of the reading is that
   a. Raymond Kroc is the most successful fast-food business owner in the world.
   b. social and economic changes affect eating habits.
   c. Americans in general eat either junk food or natural food.

7. An idea implied but not directly stated in the reading is that
   a. divorce causes people to change their eating habits.
   b. many married women began to work in the 1960s.
   c. natural foods are still popular today.

8. Which of the following did not contribute to Raymond Kroc's success?
   a. his partnership with the McDonald brothers
   b. the back-to-nature movement
   c. a changing economy

9. A social movement not mentioned in the reading is
   a. the hippie movement.
   b. the back-to-nature movement.
   c. the women's liberation movement.

10. The best alternative title for this reading would be
    a. Lifestyles in the United States.
    b. Factors Influencing the American Diet.
    c. The American Fast Food Business.

WRITING Student Course Book p. 50

Has the diet in your country changed much during the last thirty years? What is your country's version of "fast food"? When do people eat traditional dishes and when do they eat "fast food"?

Discuss these questions in class and then write a paragraph about food in your country.

Circle the best answer.

1. I'd like _____ coffee, please.
   a. a bowl of
   b. a pound of
   c. a glass of

2. Would you like _____ wine or beer?
   a. a can of
   b. a jar of
   c. a glass of

3. How about _____ rye bread for your ham and cheese sandwich?
   a. a few loaves of
   b. a few pounds of
   c. a few slices of

4. I'm not very hungry. I'll just have _____ french fries with my hamburger.
   a. a pound of
   b. a small dish of
   c. a few of

5. I'd like to have _____ spaghetti and meatballs, please.
   a. a box of
   b. a bunch of
   c. an order of

6. Mr. Cleary decided to cook a special meal, and so he bought _____ chicken for his family's dinner.
   a. a piece of
   b. a package of
   c. a leg of

7. The chef used _____ lettuce to make a salad for five people.
   a. a piece of
   b. a head of
   c. a slice of

8. Could I have _____ milk to drink with this cookie, please?
   a. a glass of
   b. a quart of
   c. a gallon of

9. Let's get _____ strawberry jelly to go with these two muffins.
   a. a case of
   b. a jar of
   c. a bottle of

10. The recipe called for _____ butter.
    a. a bowl of
    b. a pound of
    c. a bottle of

Circle the best answer.

1. A. Would you like to go swimming or play tennis?
    B. Oh, I think I'd _____ to play tennis.
        a. rather
        b. like
        c. rather have

2. A. How would you like your meat cooked?
    B. I'd _____ it rare, please.
        a. rather
        b. like
        c. have

3. A. Would you prefer to own a Jaguar or a Mercedes?
    B. I'd _____ a Porsche!
        a. feel like
        b. rather
        c. rather have

4. A. Would you like to go skating today?
    B. Well, I'm _____ to go out today.
        a. prefer not
        b. not feeling like
        c. not really in the mood

5. A. Do you want to watch the football game on TV?
    B. Oh, _____ watching TV right now.
        a. I really don't feel like
        b. I'd really prefer not to
        c. I don't prefer

6. A. _____ to go to the ballet with me next Saturday?
    B. Well, thanks, but I'm busy next week.
        a. Do you want
        b. Would you rather
        c. Would you prefer

7. A. _____ to study alone.
    B. Okay. I'll leave you alone.
        a. I'd prefer not to
        b. I'm really not in the mood
        c. I'd prefer

8. A. _____ leave right now?
    B. No. I don't mind staying a little longer.
        a. Do you like to
        b. Would you rather
        c. Would you

9. A. _____ have any early meetings.
    B. Okay. I'll schedule your first appointment at 11:00 A.M.
        a. I'd prefer not to
        b. I'd like to
        c. I'd prefer to

Circle the best answer.

1.   A. Do you want to meet for lunch at Joe's Diner?
     B. Sure, we _____ to Joe's in a long time.
        a. weren't
        b. didn't go
        c. haven't been

2.   A. Where _____ before you moved to Boston?
     B. In Orlando, Florida.
        a. have you lived
        b. are you living
        c. did you live

3.   A. _____ like taking a walk soon?
     B. Sure.
        a. Do you feel
        b. Have you felt
        c. Were you feeling

4.   A. What kind of work _____ with computers now?
     B. I'm doing mostly sales and marketing.
        a. have you done
        b. do you do
        c. you are doing

5.   A. What do you think of the new boss?
     B. Before I met him, I _____ a better opinion of him!
        a. had
        b. have had
        c. was having

6.   A. _____ the dessert?
     B. Yes, it was delicious.
        a. Were you liking
        b. Did you like
        c. Have you liked

7.   A. How long _____ since you got your hair cut?
     B. About four months.
        a. have you been
        b. will it be
        c. has it been

8.   A. Do you believe it? Just before I left, it _____ to rain and I didn't have an umbrella.
     B. That's too bad!
        a. has started
        b. started
        c. is starting

9.   A. Why _____ like going dancing?
     B. I wasn't in the mood.
        a. didn't you feel
        b. don't you feel
        c. do you feel

Circle the best answer.

1. My husband
    | |
    | a. wants them |
    | b. wants |
    | c. prefers us |

    to move, but I want to stay here.

2. His parents
    | |
    | a. want |
    | b. want him |
    | c. want them |

    to study more, but he prefers to go to parties.

3. The President
    | |
    | a. prefers to |
    | b. wants |
    | c. would rather |

    Congress to raise taxes.

4. His wife
    | |
    | a. prefers him |
    | b. rather he |
    | c. wants him |

    to open up a savings account.

5. The negotiators
    | |
    | a. want |
    | b. would rather |
    | c. want it |

    more time to work out a compromise.

6. The manager
    | |
    | a. would rather |
    | b. will want you |
    | c. will want it |

    to give a report of your findings.

7. The car dealer
    | |
    | a. wants me |
    | b. wants |
    | c. prefers |

    to make up my mind by the end of the week.

8. The Internal Revenue Service
    | |
    | a. would rather |
    | b. wants me |
    | c. prefers I |

    to make copies of my income tax forms from last year.

9. The customers
    | |
    | a. want the restaurant |
    | b. want |
    | c. prefer |

    to expand, but the owner doesn't want to.

10. Dr. Peters
    | |
    | a. wanted him |
    | b. wanted |
    | c. wanted her |

    to have another operation, but Mrs. Clark didn't want her husband to have any more surgery.

Listen and decide *where the conversation takes place.* Circle the best answer.

Example   You will hear: A. Where do you want to go to dinner after this class?
                               B. Oh, I don't care.

                Answer: a. in a restaurant
                          ⓑ. in a classroom
                           c. at someone's home

1. a. at someone's home
    b. at a Chinese restaurant
    c. at an Italian restaurant

2. a. at a pet store
    b. at a florist
    c. at someone's home

3. a. in the dining room
    b. in the study
    c. in the bathroom

4. a. at someone's home
    b. at a liquor store
    c. at a restaurant

5. a. at a political meeting
    b. at a gas station
    c. at someone's home

6. a. at a diner
    b. in someone's kitchen
    c. at a lake

7. a. in a taxi cab
    b. in an office
    c. at a tennis court

8. a. in a paint store
    b. at someone's home
    c. in a boat

GRAMMAR CHECK: *WH-Ever Words*   Student Course Book p. 54

Circle the best answer.

1. A. What time do you want to go home?

    B. | a. Whatever |
        | b. Wherever | you want to leave is okay with me.
        | c. Whenever |

2. A. Who does she want me to tell?

    B. She wants you to tell her secretary | a. whenever |
                                            | b. whoever | you can.
                                            | c. wherever |

3. A. What should I do with the car?

    B. You should park it | a. whatever |
                           | b. wherever | you find a space.
                           | c. however |

4. A. Who makes the decisions about the investments for the company?

    B. The president does | a. whatever |
                           | b. whoever | she thinks is best.
                           | c. however |

For each of the following dialogs, circle the most appropriate line for Speaker B.

1. A. Would you mind if I took you home early?
   B. a. It isn't up to you.
      b. It doesn't make any difference to me.
      c. It's for me to feel strongly about.

2. A. How would you like to go swimming today?
   B. a. It's entirely your matter.
      b. I would matter.
      c. I don't care. It's for you to decide.

3. A. Would it disturb you if I turned on the baseball game?
   B. a. No, I wouldn't mind.
      b. No, it's entirely your preference.
      c. No, it's all the same.

4. A. Would it bother you if I had a cigar?
   B. a. The decision doesn't matter.
      b. It doesn't make any difference to me.
      c. It would disturb you.

5. A. Do you have any preference about the choice of wine?
   B. a. It's entirely up to you.
      b. It's the same decision to me.
      c. It doesn't matter to me whether you drink or not.

6. A. Do you have any strong feelings about my growing a beard?
   B. a. It doesn't mind me.
      b. I don't care one way or the other.
      c. It's for you.

7. A. If you'd rather I drop you off here, I will.
   B. a. I don't feel strongly.
      b. It's entirely yours.
      c. It doesn't make any difference.

8. A. Would it disturb you if I turned on the rock-and-roll station?
   B. a. No. I'd rather you make the decision.
      b. No. It's entirely disturbing.
      c. No. It doesn't matter to me.

9. A. Do you care whether or not we see a science fiction movie?
   B. a. No. It's your decision.
      b. No. I don't have any feelings.
      c. No. It's whether or not you go.

10. A. Would you mind if I made spaghetti instead of noodles?
    B. a. No. It doesn't matter whether or not.
       b. No. I don't care about the one way or the other.
       c. No. I don't feel strongly about it one way or the other.

Listen and circle the answer that is *closest in meaning* to the sentence you have heard.

Example   You will hear: I guess I'd rather have the tomato soup.

                 Answer: a.   My guest would like tomato soup.
                            (b.) I prefer the tomato soup.
                             c.   I don't care about the tomato soup.

1. a.   I would like fresh vegetables and salad with my meal.
    b.   Today's choice features our fresh vegetable salad.
    c.   You can have either fresh vegetables or salad.

2. a.   What would you like to eat now?
    b.   Are you ready to order?
    c.   I want you to order for me now.

3. a.   Could you please bring some rolls and butter?
    b.   Would you like some rolls and butter?
    c.   How would you like your rolls and butter?

4. a.   Do you have any white wine?
    b.   Where's my glass of white wine?
    c.   I'd like some white wine.

5. a.   I can't see the special.
    b.   What's the special?
    c.   Hmm . . . I guess I'll have the special.

6. a.   I'd rather have white meat.
    b.   I would like dark meat, not white meat, please.
    c.   This meat is darker than that meat.

7. a.   That selection was recommended.
    b.   Would you recommend that selection?
    c.   There are so many things to choose from. Can you recommend something for me?

8. a.   Did you have an appetizer?
    b.   Do you want an appetizer?
    c.   How would you like your appetizer?

9. a.   Even if you don't have the special, you get salad.
    b.   I don't know whether or not you should order the salad.
    c.   Order the special. Then, you'll get a salad.

10. a.   Is the French or Italian dressing better?
    b.   Would you like French and Italian dressing?
    c.   Do you want French or Italian dressing?

I. For each of the following dialogs, circle the most appropriate line for Speaker A.

1. A. a. Would you prefer Mt. Everest?
        b. Would you be interested in climbing Mt. Everest with me?
        c. How do you like Mt. Everest?
    B. No thanks. I'm not really crazy about heights!

2. A. a. I didn't hear you.
        b. It's too big.
        c. That was quite a meal!
    B. Thanks for saying so.

3. A. a. Joan is always playing loud music.
        b. How did you like the music?
        c. Could you possibly turn down the music?
    B. It wasn't as good as I thought it would be.

4. A. a. Are you with me so far?
        b. I'm annoyed with you.
        c. Would you mind repeating that?
    B. Let me see. I think so.

5. A. a. How do you like this couch?
        b. What seems to be the problem with the couch?
        c. Would you mind moving the couch?
    B. It's just what I had in mind.

6. A. a. How would you like me to cook your hamburger?
        b. I was a little disappointed.
        c. I missed that.
    B. Oh, I don't care.

7. A. a. Why don't you talk to him about it?
        b. Do you follow me?
        c. I'm furious with you.
    B. I guess I should.

8. A. a. Would you mind if I left work early today?
        b. Are you satisfied with your new job?
        c. What do you think of your new job?
    B. It's your decision.

II. For each of the following dialogs, circle the most appropriate line for Speaker B.

1. A. I thought your singing was excellent.
    B. a. I didn't get that.
        b. I really don't enjoy singing very much.
        c. It's nice of you to say so.

2. A. Let's go into the city for dinner.
    B. a. Is it expensive enough?
        b. It's very nice of you to say that.
        c. I'm tired of going into the city.

(continued)

3. A. When do you want to go shopping?
   B. a. I'm glad you like it.
      b. Whenever you want is fine with me.
      c. Oh, come on!

4. A. Do you by any chance know where the nearest drug store is?
   B. a. Have you got all that?
      b. What did you say? I'm lost.
      c. Sure. Walk two blocks and it's on the right.

5. A. Would you like to exchange this for another one?
   B. a. No. I didn't hear you.
      b. I don't think so.
      c. No. I'm sick of refunds.

6. A. Would you rather walk?
   B. a. You're just saying that.
      b. No. I'd prefer to take a taxi.
      c. It's fine.

III. Circle the best answer.

1. I'm _____ watching TV.
   a. looking at
   b. pleased with
   c. tired of

2. Well, _____ I was a little tired, so I fell asleep.
   a. to tell you the truth
   b. let me see if
   c. go on

3. I wouldn't want it _____ smaller.
   a. any
   b. so
   c. too

4. Could you _____ tell me when the next train leaves?
   a. mind to
   b. by any chance
   c. seem to

5. _____ see if I understand.
   a. Do you
   b. Could you
   c. Let me

6. Would you be _____ buying a new dishwasher?
   a. constantly
   b. interested in
   c. honestly

7

I. Choose the best preposition to form a two-word verb with the verbs below. Circle your answer.

1. rely _____
    a. down
    b. out
    c. on

2. depend _____
    a. in
    b. on
    c. of

3. pick _____
    a. back
    b. down
    c. up

4. count _____
    a. on
    b. into
    c. of

5. bring _____
    a. of
    b. back
    c. at

6. drop _____
    a. off
    b. at
    c. up

7. put _____
    a. on
    b. of
    c. at

8. run _____
    a. into
    b. in
    c. at

9. break _____
    a. under
    b. down
    c. at

10. turn _____
    a. on
    b. of
    c. at

II. Choose the best two-word verb from above to complete the following sentences. There may be more than one answer for each question.

1. Michael _____ his best suit for his first job interview yesterday.

2. Mary called the furniture store to see when she could _____ her new sofa.

3. The President has great faith in you. He knows he can _____ you.

4. There's a great movie on tonight. Let's _____ the television.

5. I need my typewriter back so I can type my history paper. When can you _____

    it _____ to me?

6. Do you ever _____ your old friend Sam anymore?

7. I'm afraid this old car is in bad condition. I'm worried that it's going to _____

8. I have to _____ this book _____ at the library before

    we go home, okay?

I. You and your spouse are nervous parents. Your son is about to go off to college alone and you are very concerned about leaving him on his own for the first time. Write an appropriate question with *will* for each of the following answers.

1. _____
    Yes, I'll call you every week.

2. _____
    No, I won't be lonely.

3. _____
    Yes, I give you my word that I'll study hard.

4. _____
    Yes, I promise not to get into any trouble!

5. _____
    Yes, Mom and Dad, I'll miss you!

II. Write an appropriate contraction using *will* for the following sentences.

Example   Mr. Phillips promises ___he'll___ take good care of our dog while we're away.

1. Dr. Stone, how much longer do you think _____ be before the operation is finished?

2. By this time next week, _____ be on my way to Hawaii.

3. _____ feel a little pain at first, but then you _____ feel anything.

4. My son loves children. I'm sure _____ make a great father.

5. The boss told us _____ all be getting raises next month.

6. Edward and Betty want to buy a house next year. _____ need a loan from the bank in order to afford it.

7. Promise me _____ be nice to my new boyfriend, Dad.

8. I know _____ be a great party.

Listen and decide what the relationship between the two speakers is. Circle the best answer.

Example   You will hear: A.   I promise I'll return the car by five o'clock.
                               B.   Okay. You don't have to hurry home.

                 Answer: a.   teacher–student
                           ⓑ   parent–teenager
                             c.   car dealer–customer

1.   a.   doctor–patient
     b.   principal–student
     c.   employee–employer

2.   a.   mother–father
     b.   tailor–customer
     c.   pet store owner–customer

3.   a.   editor–journalist
     b.   boyfriend–girlfriend
     c.   judge–lawyer

4.   a.   supermarket owner–cashier
     b.   customer–waiter
     c.   actor–director

5.   a.   taxi driver–passenger
     b.   flight attendant–pilot
     c.   train conductor–passenger

6.   a.   student–student
     b.   store owner–customer
     c.   typewriter salesman–secretary

7.   a.   mother–child
     b.   dentist–nurse
     c.   student–teacher

8.   a.   clothing store manager–sales clerk
     b.   bartender–cashier
     c.   head librarian–assistant

FUNCTIONS   Student Course Book p. 63

Circle the best answer.

1.   Can I _____ you to drive the car
     safely?
     a.   guarantee
     b.   depend on
     c.   be sure

2.   I'm _____ on you to listen to the
     weather report tonight.
     a.   promising
     b.   guaranteeing
     c.   counting

3.   Don't worry! I won't _____.
     a.   be sure
     b.   disappoint you
     c.   give you my word

4.   I _____ you'll be happy with
     your new hairstyle.
     a.   assure
     b.   rely
     c.   promise

5.   You can _____ depend on Bob.
     He's very bright.
     a.   be sure of
     b.   positive
     c.   definitely

6.   I'll try not to _____.
     a.   assure you
     b.   be sure
     c.   let you down

7.   You should _____ your own
     instincts.
     a.   rely on
     b.   depend
     c.   guarantee

8.   She says she will _____ me a
     position on the committee for next year.
     a.   let
     b.   assure
     c.   rely

A warranty is the basic agreement between a buyer and a seller: The buyer gives money in exchange for an item the seller guarantees will work. So, for example, when you buy an expensive item such as a camera, a refrigerator, or a car, you want to get your money's worth. You shop around until you find the one that best suits your needs. You listen carefully to the salesperson's "pitch." Chances are he or she will tell you that a certain product is the best that money can buy. A smart shopper evaluates the features of a product carefully and determines what guarantees the dealer or manufacturer offers.

When you finally purchase the item and bring it home, you should put the product warranty in a safe place, in case something goes wrong. Occasionally, a company requires the customer to send in a registration card before the warranty goes into effect. Be sure to fill this out and send it in, or the company may not honor your warranty.

There are two types of warranties: full and limited. A full warranty guarantees that the manufacturer will repair or replace an item or refund the money paid for it if it is defective. A limited warranty states that the manufacturer will repair defective parts of an item, but you usually have to take or mail it back to the manufacturer, pay labor charges, and include money for return shipping and handling costs. Both full and limited warranties have time limits, guarantee only certain parts of the product, and do not cover damage caused by neglect or misuse.

Making a big purchase is always risky business, but less so if you keep these things in mind: Shop around and compare brands and prices, ask about the warranty before you buy a product, send in the registration card, and hold on to that warranty!

I. Circle the best answer.

1. If you want to "get your money's worth,"
    a. you don't want to spend too much money.
    b. you want to spend a lot of money.
    c. you want a quality product.

2. An item that "suits your needs" is
    a. a suit that you need.
    b. one that has all the features you want.
    c. one that never needs repair.

3. You get a warranty "in case something goes wrong," such as when
    a. the camera you buy malfunctions.
    b. you forget to buy a case.
    c. you take home the wrong camera.

4. When you "shop around" you
    a. walk around the shop.
    b. go to several stores.
    c. shop in your neighborhood.

5. "Chances are the warranty on a cheap item isn't very good" is the same as saying
    a. you won't get a chance to use it.
    b. there's a chance there is no warranty.
    c. it probably doesn't guarantee much.

II. Match the sentences.

a. If a company doesn't honor a warranty,

b. If your camera accidentally falls into a swimming pool,

c. When you send an item to a company for repair,

d. If you buy a used car from someone you don't know,

e. When a salesperson gives you a "pitch,"

1. _____ return shipping costs must be paid.

2. _____ it is risky business.

3. _____ it is often difficult to resist buying.

4. _____ it won't repair or replace a product.

5. _____ it is not covered in the warranty.

WRITING

Student Course Book pp. 64–65

Choose one of the following situations and write a letter to the company or individual. Complain about the defective product or the inconvenience it has caused you, remind them of the terms of their warranty or agreement, and ask for a refund or replacement.

1. It's summer and you have just bought a new air conditioner. There was a terrible storm a few days ago and the air conditioner hasn't worked since.

2. You went on vacation and rented a car for a week. The car broke down in a small town, and by the time it was repaired, your vacation was over. The rental agency would not refund your money, but they offered to let you have the car for another week. You were expected back at work, so you couldn't take advantage of their offer.

3. You hired a photographer for your wedding. He took a lot of pictures, but they all turned out too dark. The photographer won't charge you for the pictures, but he will charge you for his time.

4. You bought a watch that was supposed to be waterproof. You wore it on a scuba diving expedition and it stopped working.

When you have finished writing your letter, exchange letters with a classmate. Answer your classmate's letter, telling why you will or will not honor the request.

Circle the best answer.

1. Anne and Bob intend | a. to get / b. getting | married in May.

2. Jody decided | a. to design / b. designing | a new industrial robot.

3. We enjoyed | a. to listen / b. listening | to the jazz concert last night.

4. My parents are thinking of | a. buying / b. to buy | a condominium.

5. The President is preparing | a. giving / b. to give | an important speech to Congress.

6. Uncle Charlie finally agreed | a. giving up / b. to give up | gambling.

7. The little boy admitted | a. to stealing / b. to steal | the box of candy from the store.

8. I believe in | a. jogging / b. to jog | every day in order to prevent heart failure.

9. When he heard the 5:00 P.M. bell, the factory worker stopped | a. working. / b. to work. |

10. Would you consider | a. to go / b. going | to a museum with me today?

11. The stock broker expects | a. to see / b. seeing | an increase in the stock's value.

12. The bird was hopping on one foot. It seemed | a. to be / b. being | hurt.

13. The scientist is planning | a. beginning / b. to begin | a new experiment on alcoholism.

14. The prisoner hopes | a. getting out / b. to get out | of jail within a few months.

15. The police officer denied | a. to accept / b. accepting | the bribe.

16. My doctor suggested | a. to take / b. taking | a vacation.

For each of the following dialogs, circle the most appropriate line for Speaker B.

1. A. Pam, what are you doing tonight?
    B. a. I'd be happy to.
        b. I'm not likely.
        c. I don't know yet.

2. A. Would you like to join me in going to a rock concert?
    B. a. Sure. I'd be exciting.
        b. Thanks. I'd love to.
        c. Sure. I'm like that.

3. A. Does the show start at 9:00 or 10:00?
    B. a. I'm not certain.
        b. I'm probably sure.
        c. It's most likely.

4. A. Would you be interested in going scuba diving with me?
    B. a. Sure. Going scuba diving sounds exciting.
        b. Sure. I'm certainly going to.
        c. Sure. I'd most likely love to do that.

5. A. So, you're definitely going to move to Alaska?
    B. a. Yes, I've thought about it for a long time.
        b. Yes, I've intended it.
        c. Yes, I've given it a lot.

6. A. What have you decided to do?
    B. a. I've intended to join the tennis team.
        b. I intend to join the tennis team.
        c. I've gone to the tennis team.

◻▭ LISTENING   Student Course Book p. 67

Circle the best response to Speaker A.

Example   You will hear: Hi! It's me.

                 Answer: a. How about you?
                          ⓑ Oh, hi! How's everything?
                           c. Fine.

1. a. Fine, thanks.   4. a. Good. I'll be interested.
    b. I'd love to.   b. Okay. I'll see you then.
    c. I'm not sure.   c. I'll most likely be there.

2. a. Well, I'm not.   5. a. Wow! Going to have fun!
    b. Good!   b. Boy! Go to run! How about that!
    c. Sure, I'd be happy to.   c. Gee! Running in a race! I can't believe it!

3. a. I'm going to read a book. 6. a. You know.
    b. I don't know yet.   b. Probably.
    c. I'm going to be fine.   c. What is it?

I. Circle the best answer.

1. I've _____ buying a BMW.
   a. thinking of
   b. been thinking about
   c. might be

2. Maybe you _____ talk to the bank to ask for a loan.
   a. might
   b. will most likely
   c. should

3. I'm _____ I want to leave my sick child home alone.
   a. happy
   b. thinking
   c. not sure

4. Barbara intends _____ become a doctor.
   a. of
   b. about
   c. to

5. I _____ I'll try to quit eating sweets.
   a. thought
   b. guess
   c. consider

6. The judge has _____ a lot of thought.
   a. given it
   b. thought about
   c. been thinking

7. Sally _____ break up with Chuck soon.
   a. thinks about
   b. plans to
   c. doesn't know yet to

8. I've _____ ask Larry to marry me.
   a. been thinking to
   b. decided to
   c. thought I

II. For each of the following dialogs, circle the most appropriate line for Speaker B.

1. A. What have you and Richard decided to do?
   B. a. We may.
      b. We're not certain.
      c. We've been thinking of it.

2. A. Would you like to join me? I'm having lunch downtown.
   B. a. Well, I thought I might stay in the office and eat at my desk.
      b. I'm thinking about eating lunch.
      c. I don't like that.

3. A. I've been thinking about wearing my blue suit to the party.
   B. a. I'll let you know.
      b. I'm not sure.
      c. Really? I thought I'd wear a tuxedo.

4. A. Are you going to fire him soon?
   B. a. Promise?
      b. I'm most likely not sure.
      c. Well, I thought I'd give him one more chance.

5. A. When are you going to buy your new word processor?
   B. a. I thought I'd buy it.
      b. I may think about it tomorrow.
      c. I may buy it tomorrow.

Listen to the conversation and decide whether Speaker B's plan of action is "definite," "probable," or "possible." Circle your answer.

Example   You will hear: A.   What are you going to do tonight?
                                B.   I'm not sure. I might go to a movie.

                 Answer: a.   definite
                            b.   probable
                            ©   possible

1. a. definite   6. a. definite
    b. probable   b. probable
    c. possible   c. possible

2. a. definite   7. a. definite
    b. probable   b. probable
    c. possible   c. possible

3. a. definite   8. a. definite
    b. probable   b. probable
    c. possible   c. possible

4. a. definite   9. a. definite
    b. probable   b. probable
    c. possible   c. possible

5. a. definite   10. a. definite
    b. probable   b. probable
    c. possible   c. possible

Listen and circle the answer that is *closest in meaning* to the sentences you have heard.

1. a. I'm going to make an apple pie tonight.
    b. Tonight's dessert is apple pie.
    c. I may make an apple pie for dessert.

2. a. I'm not taking Chinese.
    b. I'm thinking of studying Chinese.
    c. I'm learning Chinese.

3. a. I made my father a sweater for his birthday.
    b. My father thought I made him a sweater for his birthday.
    c. I'm thinking of making a sweater for my father's birthday.

4. a. I might leave early today.
    b. I made him go home early today.
    c. May I go home early today?

5. a. Ruth might ask me to the prom.
    b. I think Ruth asked me to the prom.
    c. I might ask Ruth to the prom.

6. a. I want to change my major.
    b. I'm thinking of changing my job.
    c. I've decided to change my job.

Circle the best answer.

1. I _____ clean up my room in a few minutes.
    a. was going
    b. intended
    c. thought I would

2. I'll do my taxes _____.
    a. as soon
    b. the first chance
    c. right away

3. The brownies should be checked _____.
    a. a little while
    b. a little later
    c. a while

4. I _____ wash the dishes after dinner.
    a. was planning to
    b. thought of
    c. intend

5. She promised she'd pick up the tickets _____.
    a. the first chance she got
    b. as soon as I can
    c. in a little later

6. I _____ to mail the letter yesterday, but I forgot to buy stamps.
    a. am planning
    b. intend
    c. was planning

7. I don't mind leaving now. I'll take you home _____.
    a. in a little while
    b. right away
    c. the first chance I get

8. I _____ wait until tomorrow to call my insurance agent about the car.
    a. am thinking of
    b. was thinking to
    c. thought I would

GRAMMAR CHECK: *Questions with the Present Perfect*   Student Course Book p. 69

Write an appropriate question for the following answers.

1. A. _____

    B. No, I haven't. I was planning to make the beds right away.

2. A. _____

    B. No, I haven't done my homework yet. I'll do it as soon as I can.

3. A. _____

    B. Yes, I've made those copies you wanted.

4. A. _____

    B. No, I haven't received the telephone bill yet. I should get it soon.

5. A. _____

    B. No, Linda hasn't given her speech yet. She's supposed to give it a little later.

6. A. _____

    B. No, I haven't typed your paper yet. I thought I'd get to it in a little while.

Circle the best answer.

1. Hi, Scott! How _____ been?
   a. had you
   b. have you
   c. are you

2. Last time I saw you, you _____ to become a musician.
   a. plan
   b. were planning
   c. have been planning

3. I _____ I was a dreamer.
   a. guessed
   b. was guessing
   c. guess

4. About four years ago I _____ to become a doctor.
   a. have decided
   b. will have decided
   c. decided

5. I _____ you said you were going to become a movie star.
   a. have thought
   b. thought
   c. am thinking

6. Well, my new idea is that I _____ go into financial consulting.
   a. have gone to
   b. am going to
   c. will go to

7. A lot _____ since we last met.
   a. have happened
   b. has happened
   c. is happening

8. Yes. We _____ lunch together soon.
   a. should have
   b. should have had
   c. shouldn't have

FUNCTIONS   Student Course Book pp. 70–71

For each of the following dialogs, circle the most appropriate line for Speaker B.

1. A. What are you doing this afternoon?
   B. a. You can depend on me.
      b. I'd love to.
      c. I've been thinking of going to the beach.

2. A. Do you promise to do your homework soon?
   B. a. I'd like that.
      b. Absolutely.
      c. I agree.

3. A. I'm very disappointed with my new job.
   B. a. That's too bad.
      b. Can I depend on that?
      c. Promise?

4. A. I'm going out for a drink. Would you like to join me?
   B. a. I'd be happy to.
      b. You can say that again!
      c. Wow!

5. A. Can I depend on you to call me tomorrow?
   B. a. You're right.
      b. I give you my word.
      c. I've thought about it for a long time.

8

For each of the following dialogs, circle the best answer for Speaker B.

1. A. Do you want me to sweep the floor?
    B. a. For a change.
        b. That's nice.
        c. No. That's all right.

2. A. Oh, no! I'm late and I still haven't walked the dog.
    B. a. Do you want me?
        b. I'll be glad.
        c. I'll be happy to walk him, if you'd like.

3. A. Would you like me to type that for you?
    B. a. No. Listen!
        b. No. That's not nice.
        c. No. Don't worry about it.

4. A. Let me do the laundry for once. You're always doing it.
    B. a. Okay. I'd appreciate that offer.
        b. Okay. That would be very nice of you.
        c. Okay. Don't worry about it.

5. A. Thank you for offering, Tom, but I don't mind vacuuming.
    B. a. No, really! You're always the one who vacuums.
        b. No! I'd appreciate that.
        c. No! Come! You're always vacuuming.

Listen and circle the best answer.

Example   You will hear: A. Do you want me to erase the board?
                             B. No. That's okay. I don't mind erasing it.

                  Answer: a. They are in a classroom.
                            b. They are in a bank.
                            c. They are racing by the diving board.

1. a. Mrs. Crawford and Sally are driving in a car.
    b. Mrs. Crawford and Sally are closing the store at the end of the day.
    c. Mrs. Crawford and Sally are opening the store at the beginning of the day.

2. a. Bob and Mike are going to drive together.
    b. Bob and Mike don't like to drive to work together.
    c. Bob and Mike are not going to drive together today.

3. a. Richard always feeds the baby.
    b. Richard is going to change the baby.
    c. Richard is going to feed the baby.

4. a. John doesn't want Linda to go shopping.
    b. John doesn't like shopping.
    c. John wants Linda to go shopping.

5. a. Mr. Jones is glad Jack will write the memo.
    b. Jack is not going to write the memo.
    c. Mr. Jones is not going to write the memo.

Circle the best answer.

1. The oil in my car _____ in a long time.
   a. hasn't been changed
   b. has been changed
   c. is being changed

2. _____, in time for the party?
   a. Will the windows be fixed
   b. Have the windows fixed
   c. Are the windows fixed

3. The living room walls _____ by that time.
   a. have just been painted
   b. will have just been painted
   c. are painted

4. The world record for long-distance running _____ at the Olympics last summer.
   a. is being broken
   b. has been broken
   c. was broken

5. My eyes _____ since I was fifteen years old.
   a. weren't examined
   b. haven't been examined
   c. will not have been examined

6. The floors _____ right now, sir.
   a. had been swept
   b. are being swept
   c. have been swept

7. The hamster _____ twice yesterday.
   a. was fed
   b. has been fed
   c. wasn't been fed

8. Last year at this time, the rocket _____ for the first time.
   a. is being launched
   b. was being launched
   c. will be launched

LISTENING   Student Course Book p. 75

Listen and circle the best response to Speaker A.

Example   You will hear: I see you're cleaning out the attic. Do you want any help?

                Answer: a. Sure. If I don't mind.
                           b. Sure. You don't mind.
                       c. Sure. If you don't mind.

1. a. Sure. I'd be glad to.
   b. Sure. Give you a hand.
   c. Sure. If it's no trouble.

2. a. If you wouldn't mind.
   b. No, if you mind.
   c. No trouble.

3. a. Yes. I'd be happy.
   b. No. I'd appreciate it.
   c. No. I'd be glad to lend a hand.

4. a. Thanks. It's nice of you to offer.
   b. Thanks. I'd be happy to.
   c. Thanks. I'd be glad to lend a hand.

5. a. Oh, come on!
   b. No. That's okay.
   c. Sure. Don't mind.

6. a. Well, do you need a hand?
   b. Well, can I give something?
   c. Well, do you mind any help?

7. a. I'd be glad to trouble you.
   b. Can I hand it to you?
   c. Do you want a hand?

8. a. Thanks. If it wouldn't mind.
   b. Thanks. If it's no trouble.
   c. Thanks. You would be nice.

Listen and circle the answer that is *closest in meaning* to the sentence you have heard.

Example You will hear: Would you like me to carry those books for you, Fred?

Answer: ⓐ Let me carry those books for you, Fred.
b. It's nice of you to offer to carry those books, Fred.
c. Fred, give me those books!

1. a. I want some help with the positioning of that picture.
   b. I'm happy I could help you with the positioning of that picture.
   c. Let me help you adjust the position of that picture.

2. a. I accept your offer of help.
   b. That's okay. I can do it myself.
   c. Come on! I need your help.

3. a. Look at this dirty basement!
   b. Look! Your sister wants to help you clean the basement.
   c. Look! I'm going to help you clean the basement.

4. a. All right. But I don't want to inconvenience you.
   b. All right. Help me, but don't bother me.
   c. Thanks, but I don't want you to get into trouble.

5. a. Oh, no. You're in trouble. Lend me a hand.
   b. It's not inconvenient for me. i'm glad to help you.
   c. Oh, I'm not too happy about troubling you.

6. a. Chopping all those carrots doesn't make any sense.
   b. There's no reason for you to chop carrots.
   c. You shouldn't have to cut all those carrots alone.

Circle the best answer.

1. _____ help you put up those posters?
   a. Do you want to
   b. I'd be glad to
   c. Would you like me to

2. There's no _____ for you to carry that box of records by yourself.
   a. sense
   b. reason
   c. help

3. No. Really. _____ of you to offer, but I'll fix my bike by myself.
   a. Thanks
   b. I'm glad
   c. It's nice

4. _____! I insist on helping you load the truck.
   a. Help
   b. Come on
   c. Thanks

5. Well, if you insist. But I really don't want to _____.
   a. bother
   b. put you anywhere
   c. trouble you

6. Would you like _____ cutting that wood?
   a. any help
   b. me to
   c. me to help

7. Oh. That's okay, but _____.
   a. I appreciate
   b. it's nice of you to offer
   c. there's no bother

8. Well. If you really want to help, you can, but I don't want _____.
   a. to put you in
   b. to inconvenience you
   c. to bother me

Listen carefully for specific details in each conversation. At the end of each conversation, you will be asked a question about what was said. Circle the best answer.

Example   You will hear: A. Hello. May I help you?
                                B. Yes. I'm looking for a food processor for my father. He loves to cook, and it's his birthday tomorrow.
                                A. I'm afraid we're out of food processors.
                                B. Oh, that's too bad!
                                A. But we expect some in by next week.
                                B. Hmm. I'm afraid that's too late. I need it by tomorrow. Thanks anyway.

                                What was the customer looking for?

                Answer: a. a word processor for her father's birthday next week
                            b. a food processor for her father's birthday next week
                            ©. a food processor for her father's birthday tomorrow

1. a. He wants the exercise.
    b. He wants to change the dog's habits.
    c. He wants to do Patty a favor.

2. a. in a florist shop
    b. in Vicky's backyard
    c. in Vicky's house

3. a. five pounds
    b. fifteen pounds
    c. fifty pounds

4. a. Flexible Flyers aren't made anymore.
    b. The customer was at the wrong store.
    c. The stockroom of the store was empty.

5. a. size 13 brown leather shoes
    b. size 30 black leather shoes
    c. size 13 black leather shoes

6. a. birds
    b. dogs, cats, fish, and birds
    c. dogs, cats, fish, and hamsters

FUNCTIONS   Student Course Book p. 78

For each of the dialogs, circle the most appropriate line for Speaker A.

1. A. a. Are you just looking?
        b. Can I help look?
        c. May I assist you?
    B. No. Not right now, thanks. I'm just looking.

2. A. a. Is there something in gold?
        b. Is there anything in particular I can help you find?
        c. Are you looking for a gold tie clip?
    B. Well, I'm actually looking for a gold tie clip.

3. A. a. I'm afraid these tie clips are all out of stock.
        b. We don't run out of tie clips.
        c. We're running out of gold.
    B. Oh, that's too bad. I need one for tonight.

4. A. a. Please let me know if I can be of any further assistance.
        b. If I can't assist you, please hesitate and call me.
        c. Please feel free to assist me.
    B. Okay. Thanks very much.

5. A. a. Is there any further assistance?
        b. Is there anything in particular?
        c. Is there anything else I can help you with?
    B. I guess not, but thanks anyway.

6. A. a. We're out of convertibles. Sorry.
        b. I'm afraid we don't have any more convertibles. Try our other store.
        c. We've run out of convertibles, but we expect some by the end of the week.
    B. Okay, I'll come back then.

I. Choose the best preposition to form a two-word verb with the verbs below. Circle your answer.

1. take _____
a. at
b. down
c. under

6. sweep _____
a. out
b. on
c. in

2. knock _____
a. down
b. in
c. at

7. take _____
a. at
b. out
c. of

3. fall _____
a. around
b. off
c. at

8. help _____
a. up
b. to
c. at

4. help _____
a. in
b. about
c. out

9. set _____
a. up
b. around
c. into

5. cut _____
a. with
b. off
c. of

10. cut _____
a. from
b. at
c. down

II. Choose the best two-word verb from above to complete the meaning of the following sentences. There may be more than one answer for each question, and you may have to change the verb form.

1. Susan _____ the horse and broke her arm.

2. When we do the spring cleaning, our children always _____ us _____.

3. Do you want some help _____ that picture _____?

4. I've already asked you to _____ the garbage. Why haven't you done it?

5. John, let me _____ you _____ with your homework so we can go out tonight.

6. I was crossing Main Street when a motorcycle came along and _____ me _____.

7. This dress is too long. It would be perfect if you _____ an inch from the hem.

8. We don't have enough chairs in the auditorium for tonight's lecture. We need to _____ some more.

9. I'm afraid I have to _____ that tree. It has a serious disease.

10. In the winter before we go to sleep, we _____ the ashes _____ of the fireplace.

11. Tom _____ the old woman _____ the stairs last night.

Circle the word that does not relate to the rest of the words in the group.

1. a. roller skates   b. car   c. ambulance   d. truck driver

2. a. ankle   b. knee   c. wrinkle   d. thigh

3. a. sprained   b. strained   c. fell   d. injured

4. a. mugged   b. arrested   c. robbed   d. murdered

5. a. pack up   b. take off   c. unload   d. unpack

6. a. antenna   b. fix   c. change   d. adjust

7. a. alphabetize   b. analyze   c. order   d. file

8. a. water   b. feed   c. nourish   d. liquid

9. a. hamster   b. dog   c. cat   d. animal

10. a. inconvenience   b. trouble   c. bother   d. serious

Circle the best answer.

1. Excuse me. Are you _____?
    a. very kind
    b. okay
    c. helped

2. Can I _____ to help?
    a. anything
    b. do
    c. do anything

3. Should I _____ an ambulance?
    a. help
    b. get
    c. call to

4. Glad to _____.
    a. do help
    b. mention it
    c. be of help

5. Here. Let me _____.
    a. to help you
    b. allow you
    c. help you up

6. Thanks. You're _____.
    a. very kind
    b. kind of you
    c. nice of you

7. Don't _____.
    a. be glad to help
    b. mention it
    c. problem

8. Is there _____ to help?
    a. something
    b. anything I can do
    c. no problem

Circle the best answer.

1. The boss was so happy that she
   _____.
   a. gave to him a promotion
   b. gave him a promotion
   c. gave a promotion for him

2. When are you going to _____ a
   new pair of sneakers?
   a. buy him
   b. buy for him
   c. buy with him

3. My supervisor _____ a
   wonderful recommendation.
   a. wrote me
   b. wrote to me
   c. wrote for me

4. When we were young, my father used to
   _____ bedtime stories.
   a. tell to us
   b. tell us
   c. tell for us

5. Excuse me, Mrs. Black. Could you please
   _____?
   a. pass for me the salt
   b. pass to me the salt
   c. pass me the salt

6. I needed a formal dress to wear to the prom,
   but mine was at the cleaner's. Fortunately,
   my sister had one, so she _____.
   a. lent me mine
   b. lent to me hers
   c. lent hers to me

FUNCTIONS   Student Course Book p. 80

For each of the following dialogs, circle the most appropriate line for Speaker B.

1. A. Thank you so much for lending me your TV.
   B. a. Oh. It wasn't mentioned.
      b. Oh. It was nothing.
      c. Oh. No mention.

2. A. Really! It was nice of you to help me.
   B. a. It was my doing.
      b. I'm glad I could do it.
      c. Any pleasure.

3. A. Well, here are the keys to my house on the beach. Enjoy it.
   B. a. I'm very appreciate.
      b. Thank you. I'm really very much.
      c. I really appreciate it.

4. A. You don't have to thank me. It was my pleasure to show you around the city.
   B. a. No, honestly! It was very nice of you.
      b. No. You're nice.
      c. No. I mean it! You're grateful.

5. A. Thank you so much for your hospitality. I really enjoyed myself.
   B. a. Any time.
      b. My help.
      c. I'm helpful.

Oscar, Emmy, Grammy, Tony—these sound like names of people, but actually they are awards given to entertainers in the United States each year. Each of these award ceremonies is a gala affair, usually held in Hollywood or New York. Hundreds of would-be winners dress in formal attire to triumphantly claim their prize or graciously acknowledge those who win.

The oldest of these awards is the Oscar, a small statue presented by the Academy of Motion Picture Arts and Sciences. The Academy Awards ceremony originated in 1928 in Hollywood to honor outstanding achievement in performance, photography, direction, production, music, and other areas of film-making. The name Oscar was supposedly given to the small statue in 1931 when the librarian and, later, executive director of the Academy, Margaret Herrick, remarked that it looked like her Uncle Oscar.

The Emmy is presented by the National Academy for Television Arts and Sciences to the top programs, performers, and "behind-the-scenes" people in commercial and public television. The Grammy is awarded by the National Academy of Recording Arts and Sciences and honors a variety of singers, musicians, producers, writers, technicians, and the records they have produced.

The Tony is an award that pays tribute to outstanding achievement in the theater. It was first presented in 1947 and named for a then-popular actress, Antoinette Perry. It honors the best among Broadway dramas and musicals in categories similar to those of the Oscar.

Millions of viewers watch these award ceremonies on television and are overjoyed when their favorite stars receive a prize. The candidates themselves spend weeks planning what they will wear, who they will go with, and what they will say in their acceptance speeches. Hundreds of thousands of dollars are spent on an event that is over in just a few hours. The winners take the coveted prizes home, grateful for the recognition their talent and hard work have brought them. The losers smile graciously, express how happy they are for the winners, and think to themselves, "Next year will be my turn!"

Circle the best answer.

1. A "gala affair" is one that
    a. includes dinner and dancing.
    b. people dress up for.
    c. awards prizes.

2. "Would-be winners" are those who
    a. have the possibility of winning prizes.
    b. have never won prizes.
    c. have won plenty of prizes.

3. Examples of "behind-the-scenes" people are
    a. actors and actresses.
    b. singers and musicians.
    c. camerapeople and technicians.

4. A "then-popular actress" is a person who
    a. was popular before.
    b. is popular now and then.
    c. is more popular now than before.

5. A "coveted prize" is one that
    a. is covered.
    b. everyone wants.
    c. is expensive.

6. Another title for this reading could be
    a. To Win or Not to Win.
    b. Hollywood Affairs.
    c. The Origin of Entertainment.

(continued)

7. An award not mentioned was one for
   a. directors and producers.
   b. TV shows and their stars.
   c. newspaper columnists.

8. The main idea of the reading is that
   a. too much money is spent on award ceremonies.
   b. awards are very important to both entertainers and their audience.
   c. Americans like award ceremonies.

9. On the night of the show, candidates usually
   a. stay home and watch television.
   b. wear something special.
   c. spend hundreds of thousands of dollars.

10. An idea implied but not directly stated is that
    a. award ceremonies are formal affairs.
    b. no one knows how the Oscar got its name.
    c. people are grateful when they win an award.

WRITING   Student Course Book p. 81

You are a journalist and your newspaper has assigned you to cover an award ceremony. Write an article describing the awards given, who won them, what the winners said in their acceptance speeches, who else was present at the event, and what people wore.

LISTENING   Student Course Book pp. 84–85

Listen and circle the best response to the question you have heard.

Example   You will hear: Is smoking cigarettes allowed here?

              Answer: a.   No, they aren't.
                          b.   Yes, they are.
                       ⓒ   Yes, it is.

1. a. Yes, they are.
   b. No, you aren't.
   c. Yes, it is.

2. a. No, you aren't.
   b. No, you can't.
   c. No, it isn't.

3. a. Yes, as far as I know.
   b. No, it isn't.
   c. Yes, they do.

4. a. No, you aren't.
   b. No, they aren't.
   c. No, they don't.

5. a. I don't believe it.
   b. I don't think so.
   c. No, they don't.

6. a. No, they don't.
   b. Yes, you are.
   c. Yes, it is.

7. a. No, they don't.
   b. I don't think.
   c. No, it isn't.

8. a. I believe so.
   b. No, it isn't.
   c. Yes, they are.

9. a. Yes, they do.
   b. Yes, it is.
   c. Yes, as far as I know.

10. a. No, they aren't.
    b. No, it isn't.
    c. No, they don't.

GRAMMAR CHECK: *Gerunds and Infinitives*   Student Course Book pp. 84–85

Circle the best answer.

1. Is _____ permitted here?
   a. to walk your dog
   b. walking your dog
   c. people

2. Is it okay _____ in this part of the woods?
   a. cutting down trees
   b. to cut down trees
   c. for people cutting down trees

3. Do they allow _____ in the pool after midnight?
   a. people swimming
   b. to swim
   c. swimming

4. Are people permitted _____ on the test booklet?
   a. writing
   b. to write
   c. for writing

(continued)

5. As far as you know, are _____ permitted at the tennis club?
   a. bringing guests
   b. guests
   c. to bring guests

6. Do you think _____ is allowed in this pond?
   a. people fishing
   b. to fish
   c. fishing

FUNCTIONS A   Student Course Book p. 86

For each of the following dialogs, circle the most appropriate line for Speaker A.

1. A. a. Excuse me.
      b. Pardon me, but I don't think surfing is allowed here.
      c. Excuse me, but is surfing allowed here?
   B. Oh. Thanks for telling me.

2. A. a. Do you like that! Mondays.
      b. How do you like that!
      c. Is that something!
   B. I know. I'm surprised too. I can't believe the store is closed on Mondays.

3. A. a. Is bringing floats into the water allowed here?
      b. Are floats allowed in the water here?
      c. Excuse me, but do they allow people to bring floats into the water here?
   B. Yes, they do.

4. A. a. Do you think sledding is permitted on the golf course?
      b. Well, what do you know!
      c. Isn't that something! No sledding!
   B. I don't think so.

5. A. a. Yes, it is.
      b. Is parking allowed here?
      c. There's a sign that says "No Parking," sir.
   B. Well, isn't that something!

6. A. a. Well, how do you like that.
      b. Excuse me, but do you think you're allowed to bring pets into the dorm?
      c. Pardon me, but pets aren't allowed in the dorm.
   B. Not as far as I know.

FUNCTIONS B   Student Course Book p. 86

Circle the best answer.

1. Excuse me, but I don't think _____ is allowed in the elevator.
   a. to smoke
   b. smoking
   c. you smoking

2. Well, how _____!
   a. about that
   b. do you like
   c. is that something

3. I don't think _____ to eat here.
   a. they allow
   b. you permit
   c. people are permitted

4. Are _____ allowed to ride bicycles on the sidewalks in Holland?
   a. you're
   b. people
   c. there

5. Isn't _____!
   a. people allowed here
   b. you like that
   c. that something

6. _____ me, but I think that sign says "No Flashbulbs Permitted."
   a. Allow
   b. Pardon
   c. Oh

Circle the best answer.

1. Ms. Friedman, _____ I possibly have tomorrow off?
   a. should
   b. could
   c. would

2. _____ it be possible for me to pick you up a little later than 2:00?
   a. Would
   b. Could
   c. May

3. _____ I please borrow your stereo for my party?
   a. Should
   b. May
   c. Would

4. _____ you come over to watch TV with me tonight?
   a. Maybe
   b. Should
   c. Can

5. _____ you possibly do the dishes for me tonight? I want to watch the President's speech at 7:00.
   a. Could
   b. May
   c. Shouldn't

6. He has too much work to do. He _____ possibly write that article for you by tomorrow.
   a. might
   b. couldn't
   c. shouldn't

7. _____ you should check with the nurse about that.
   a. May
   b. Will
   c. Maybe

8. I'm sure your boss _____ object to giving you a raise.
   a. could
   b. won't
   c. may

FUNCTIONS   Student Course Book p. 87

Circle the best answer.

1. _____ I ask you a favor?
   a. Maybe
   b. Would
   c. Could

2. _____ you possibly put money in the parking meter for me?
   a. Can
   b. Maybe
   c. Will

3. Let me _____.
   a. see for a minute
   b. guess so
   c. think

4. Well, I _____.
   a. suppose now
   b. don't have any mind
   c. don't see why not

5. I'm sure your parents won't _____ your driving their new car as long as you're careful.
   a. mind to
   b. object
   c. have any objection to

6. Is it _____ if I dance with your wife?
   a. possible
   b. okay with you
   c. possibly

7. I'd like to pay for dinner, if _____.
   a. that's all right with you
   b. you suppose so
   c. you don't see any reason why

8. _____ I please take a break now?
   a. Should
   b. Would
   c. May

Listen and decide what the relationship between the two speakers is. Circle the best answer.

Example You will hear: A. Would you mind if I turned up the stereo?
B. No, I wouldn't mind.

Answer: ⓐ roommate–roommate
b. student–librarian
c. surgeon–assistant

1. a. sports fan–baseball player
b. photographer–actor
c. citizen–police officer

2. a. waiter–chef
b. mother–son
c. cashier–customer

3. a. driver–passenger
b. car salesman–customer
c. diver–swimming coach

4. a. travel agent–customer
b. student–teacher
c. employee–employer

5. a. doctor–patient's wife
b. wife–husband
c. teacher–student

6. a. astronaut–astronaut
b. teacher–student
c. bride–groom

7. a. tenant–landlord
b. customer–pet store owner
c. zookeeper–visitor

8. a. guest–hotel manager
b. student–student
c. student–teacher

FUNCTIONS   Student Course Book pp. 88–89

Circle the best answer.

1. _____ I drank the rest of your orange juice?
a. Would you be all right if
b. Do you bother
c. Would it bother you if

2. No, _____ if you stayed at Peter's house tonight.
a. it's all right
b. of course
c. I wouldn't mind

3. _____. If you want to buy new skates, it's fine with me.
a. All means.
b. Certainly.
c. Don't let me stop.

4. _____ if we play one more set of tennis before we leave?
a. Is it all right
b. Would you like
c. Are you okay

5. _____ be all right if I kissed the groom?
a. Do you
b. Will you
c. Would it

6. _____ to invite Patty to join us next Sunday?
a. You'd like
b. Would you mind
c. Would you be bothered

7. _____. Ask Sarah for the car if you want to borrow it.
a. It's sure with me.
b. Go right with me.
c. By all means.

8. _____ okay with you if I stored my books in your attic?
a. Certainly
b. Would it be
c. Would you be

Match the words in the first column with their meanings in the second column.

a. allergic to   1. _____ a person who doesn't eat meat or fish

b. camera shy   2. _____ a short sleep

c. heirloom   3. _____ a round plastic disc

d. vegetarian   4. _____ a large wheel with passenger cars that turn around

e. nap   5. _____ afraid of having one's picture taken

f. to skip   6. _____ bare

g. frisbee   7. _____ sensitive to something eaten, breathed in, or touched

h. ferris wheel   8. _____ a valuable object handed down from generation to generation

i. nude   9. _____ to set up a tent outdoors

j. to camp   10. _____ to miss purposely

 LISTENING   Student Course Book p. 90

Listen to the conversations and decide whether Speaker B's response is positive or negative. Circle your answer.

Example   You will hear: A. Would you mind if I turned on the radio?
                              B. Well. I'd rather you didn't. I'm trying to study.

              Answer: a. positive
                        ⓑ negative

1. a. positive   6. a. positive
    b. negative   b. negative

2. a. positive   7. a. positive
    b. negative   b. negative

3. a. positive   8. a. positive
    b. negative   b. negative

4. a. positive   9. a. positive
    b. negative   b. negative

5. a. positive   10. a. positive
    b. negative   b. negative

John Doe, a typical American businessman, rode to work on the subway one ordinary morning. He got off at his station downtown and walked to his office building. At the entrance, a security guard was posted to check employee identification (ID) cards. John reached into his pocket, but his wallet wasn't there! He was sure he had taken it from the dresser that morning. Of course he had because it contained his subway pass, which got him on the train. John checked his other pockets, but his wallet was nowhere to be found. Someone had stolen it on the subway. His day was ruined. He couldn't even get into his own office.

For most Americans, the contents of a wallet are essential for everyday life. The wallet usually contains a driver's license, ID cards from one's job or school, credit cards, banking cards, a Social Security card, a library card, sports club or professional organization cards, and business cards, not to mention money, checks, and other important items. Having a wallet stolen represents not only a loss of money but a loss of time—perhaps time off from work—to report the theft and replace these necessary cards. A person must go through a lot of red tape and bureaucracy before his or her life returns to normal.

To get into the office, John had to call his boss and ask him to come to the security desk to vouch for him. Once in the office, John had to make numerous telephone calls to cancel his credit and banking cards and personal checks. He was put on "hold," disconnected, and told to call back later a number of times. It was a frustrating experience, but he didn't give up until he had cancelled all the cards. He didn't want anyone else spending his hard-earned money.

During lunch hour, John went to the nearest police station to fill out a report of the theft. Then he went to the bank to take out some money. He couldn't use the automated banking machine without a card, so John had to stand in line for quite a long time. At the teller's window, he didn't have any identification to show, but he did have a copy of the police report. The teller compared his signature on the report with that on his signature card in the bank files, and he was able to withdraw some money.

John took the rest of the day off to replace his picture IDs. He went to the company's Personnel Office, the Registry of Motor Vehicles, and to the university where he was taking evening courses. He didn't have to wait very long for these cards, but he did have to pay a replacement fee.

Losing a wallet can certainly be a frustrating experience. It represents not only the loss of money, but a temporary loss of identity in a society full of numbers, cards, and documents. Just as there is little we can do about a pickpocket on the subway, there is little we can do to cut through all the red tape and bureaucracy of modern times.

Circle the best answer.

1. A security guard was posted at the entrance so that
   a. he could collect employee ID cards.
   b. pickpockets wouldn't enter.
   c. people who didn't work at the office couldn't get in.

2. The contents of a person's wallet are necessary because
   a. we need money to live.
   b. they allow us to do many things.
   c. we have to buy now and pay later.

3. John's boss came to vouch for him because
   a. he had to go to the police station.
   b. the security guard had to make sure he was an employee.
   c. there were pickpockets on the subway.

4. John was "put on hold" because
   a. the person on the line couldn't talk to him at that moment.
   b. it was difficult to hold a conversation.
   c. he was holding the receiver.

5. The teller let John withdraw money from the bank because
   a. his signature matched the one on file.
   b. the police reported him.
   c. he showed his ID card.

6. John had to pay a replacement fee for some of his cards
   a. and wait several weeks for them.
   b. but he got them right away.
   c. to pay for the pictures on them.

7. When your wallet is stolen, you lose your identity because
   a. no one knows who you are.
   b. your money is gone.
   c. the cards in it are society's way of identifying you.

8. "Red tape" refers to
   a. security measures at police stations.
   b. warning signs in offices.
   c. obstacles we come up against.

9. Bureaucracy is frustrating because
   a. everything is organized into departments.
   b. there are pickpockets on the subways.
   c. we often have to cut through red tape.

10. This reading describes
    a. the modern history of American bureaucracy.
    b. how frustrating bureaucracy can be.
    c. what happened to a tourist visiting the United States.

You are writing a booklet for your country's Visitors' Bureau. In this booklet you are offering helpful hints to visitors from foreign countries. The section you are working on today is "What to Do in Case of Emergencies." Write helpful hints for each of the emergencies below.

A. To prevent the loss of your wallet, _____

_____

_____

_____

_____

B. If you lose your wallet, _____

_____

_____

_____

_____

C. If you are robbed, _____

_____

_____

_____

_____

D. If you are involved in a car accident, _____

_____

_____

_____

_____

E. If you should become seriously ill, _____

_____

_____

_____

_____

Circle the best answer to complete the following analogies in a logical way.

Example   ignite : fire *as* _____ : light
                    a.   turn off
                    ⓑ.   turn on
                    c.   build

1.   landlord : apartment *as* _____ :
     company
     a.   store
     b.   president
     c.   sublet

2.   permission : consent *as* _____ :
     approval
     a.   proof
     b.   the runaround
     c.   a go ahead

3.   alter : change *as* _____ : maintain
     a.   switch
     b.   keep up
     c.   maintenance

4.   complicated : simple *as* _____ : easy
     a.   comply
     b.   accommodate
     c.   complex

5.   freshman : first *as* _____ : last
     a.   junior
     b.   sophomore
     c.   senior

6.   make : agreement *as* sign : _____
     a.   traffic
     b.   symbol
     c.   lease

Circle the best answer.

1.   I always tell my son that he
     _____ play with matches.
     a.   must
     b.   mustn't
     c.   could

2.   Excuse me, but the sign says "No
     Swimming." You're _____ swim
     here.
     a.   mustn't
     b.   shouldn't
     c.   not supposed to

3.   Please be considerate of the other tenants.
     Your lease says that you _____
     play loud music after 11:00 P.M.
     a.   may
     b.   mustn't
     c.   can

4.   Pardon me, sir, but this is a tow-away zone.
     _____ park here.
     a.   You must
     b.   You don't have to
     c.   You aren't supposed to

5.   Class starts promptly at 9:00 A.M. You
     _____ be here by 8:55 A.M. so we
     can begin on time.
     a.   must
     b.   shouldn't
     c.   may

6.   I _____ tell you something before
     we go to the Italian restaurant. I'm allergic to
     garlic.
     a.   should
     b.   shouldn't
     c.   may

Listen and circle the answer that is *closest in meaning* to the sentence you have heard.

Example   You will hear: Wendy, could I ask you to carry these bags for me?

           Answer: a.   Wendy, I may ask you to carry these bags for me.
                     (b.)   Wendy, would you please do me a favor and carry these bags?
                     c.   Wendy, I told you carrying these bags is bad for me.

1.   a.   I'm afraid to authorize your check.
    b.   I'm sorry, but I need the bank manager's approval before I can cash your check.
    c.   I can't cash your check.

2.   a.   Was it difficult to get the loan from the bank?
    b.   Did Frank give you a hard time on the phone?
    c.   Did you have time to go to the bank for the loan?

3.   a.   Are you really subletting this apartment?
    b.   He would agree to sublet this apartment?
    c.   May I sublet this apartment?

4.   a.   Hey, are you going to build a fire?
    b.   I'm going to make a fire in the fireplace.
    c.   Is it all right to make a fire?

5.   a.   I'm not supposed to have pets.
    b.   I'm afraid pets aren't allowed in the building.
    c.   I'm sorry. No betting in the building.

6.   a.   I want to tell you I'm proud of this project.
    b.   I should tell you not to mention this project to anyone.
    c.   Please tell everyone about this project.

7.   a.   I'm sorry to complicate things, Mr. Harris, but you'll have to get your money back from another department.
    b.   I'm sorry I ran away from you, Mr. Harris. Go to the refund department, please.
    c.   You mean Mr. Harris? He's running around in the refund department.

FUNCTIONS

Circle the best answer.

1.   I'm afraid I can't install a new telephone jack without _____ of my manager.
    a.   permission
    b.   the approval
    c.   agreement

2.   Dr. Phillips, could you please _____ to enter the restricted ward of the hospital?
    a.   authorize me
    b.   approve me
    c.   agree me

3.   Did I make an adding mistake? I'm sorry, Mrs. Jones. I didn't mean to _____ for you.
    a.   make things complicated
    b.   runaround
    c.   give you hard time

4.   Guess what! Professor Thompson _____ doing research with her this summer.
    a.   agreed my
    b.   consented to my
    c.   gave the go ahead for me

5.   Could I _____ to fix my kitchen sink?
    a.   ask you
    b.   ask you a favor
    c.   possibly

6.   At Blackwell State Prison we don't _____ leave the grounds without permission.
    a.   suppose anyone
    b.   allow to
    c.   permit anyone to

I. For each of the following dialogs, circle the most appropriate line for Speaker A.

1. A. a. Would you like me to help you?
     b. I thought I might start my own consulting company.
     c. I want to thank you for taking care of my plants while I was away.
   B. Don't mention it.

2. A. a. Is it all right with you if I use the copying machine now?
     b. Here. Let me give you a hand.
     c. Could you possibly watch my bags for a minute?
   B. Oh, I don't want to trouble you.

3. A. a. Is barbecuing allowed on the beach?
     b. Could I ask you a favor?
     c. Allow me to pull out your chair.
   B. Not as far as I know.

4. A. a. I'd like to go home early, if that's okay with you.
     b. I'll probably lose my job soon. Business hasn't been good.
     c. Would it be possible for me to take a business trip to London next month?
   B. That's too bad.

5. A. a. I'm thinking of opening a restaurant in town.
     b. I don't think people are allowed to sail here.
     c. Can I count on you to give this report to the right person?
   B. Absolutely.

6. A. a. I might take a cruise down the Nile River next year.
     b. Can I help?
     c. Do you promise you'll finish your homework soon?
   B. Wow!

7. A. a. Would you like to join me?
     b. Do you prefer to go to a movie tomorrow?
     c. If you'd rather I didn't call you, I won't.
   B. I'd prefer you not to.

8. A. a. What are you watching?
     b. Have you decided what to do tonight?
     c. Would you like me to go downtown for you?
   B. I thought I'd see the Humphrey Bogart film downtown.

9. A. a. I won't let you down.
     b. May I please stay out past 11:00 tonight, Dad?
     c. I'm glad I could be of some help.
   B. It's okay with me.

10. A. a. I really appreciate it.
      b. Can I help you do that?
      c. It's nice of you to offer.
    B. If you don't mind.

II. Circle the best answer.

1. I've been thinking _____ asking Lisa to the dance.
   a. to
   b. that
   c. of

2. I'd prefer you _____ speak Spanish in our English class.
   a. don't
   b. if you didn't
   c. not to

3. There's no sense _____ when I can stay late and finish it.
   a. for you staying late
   b. your having to stay late
   c. in your staying late

4. I've given it _____, and I've decided not to quit.
   a. a long time
   b. a lot of serious thought
   c. a lot of mind

5. I'm _____ move to Florida for the winter.
   a. deciding to
   b. planning to
   c. definitely

6. Yes, _____ picnicking is allowed here at Yellowstone Park.
   a. I don't think
   b. could I ask you
   c. as far as I know

7. I can't leave early without _____ Ms. Cambell.
   a. a go ahead
   b. approving
   c. the consent of

8. I don't see _____.
   a. if it would be possible
   b. so
   c. any reason why not

9. Well, what _____! You're feeling better.
   a. do you like that
   b. do you know
   c. you know

10. Please _____ if I can be of any further assistance.
    a. don't inconvenience you
    b. don't mention it
    c. let me know

TAPE SCRIPTS FOR LISTENING EXERCISES

Page 2

Ex. I don't think we've met. My name is Joe.
1. Nice to meet you. What do you do?
2. I'm a doctor. How about you?
3. Which apartment do you live in?
4. How long have you been in the U.S.?
5. What's your major?
6. What kind of music do you like?
7. When is your baby due?
8. Whose shoes are these?

Page 3

Ex. A. Hi, John. I haven't seen you in a long time.
    B. I know. How have you been, Paul?

1. A. Hello. I don't think we've met. I'm Dr. Jones.
    B. How do you do? I'm Sam Smith. Nice to meet you.

2. A. I'm Tom. Nice to meet you.
    B. I'm pleased to meet you, too. My name is Sally.

3. A. My name's Kim. I'm from Korea. How about you?
    B. I'm Luis. I'm from Spain.

4. A. I'm an accountant. What do you do?
    B. I'm an engineer.

5. A. Tell me, Joan. How long have you been studying?
    B. Oh, for about a year.

6. A. Arthur, whose wedding are you going to?
    B. Peter's.

7. A. Lucy, what kind of music do you like?
    B. I like rock and roll.

8. A. When is your paper due, Carol?
    B. On Friday.

9. A. Which building do you live in, Bob?
    B. The tall brown one on School Street.

10. A. Ruth, whose office are you going to?
    B. Martha's.

Page 11

Ex. I have some good news.
1. That's fantastic!
2. You must be thrilled.
3. I have some bad news.
4. Oh, I'm happy to hear that.
5. You must be ecstatic.
6. Well, congratulations!
7. I'm sorry to hear that.
8. You must be very upset.

Page 11

Ex. I have some bad news.
1. I was just given a raise.
2. My parents are getting divorced.
3. I was just offered a job at Harvard University.
4. I'm going to have to shut down my business.
5. I was rejected by the business school I applied to.
6. I was awarded the prize for best violinist in the orchestra.
7. I just won the lottery.
8. I just had to pay a thousand dollars to have my car repaired.

Page 19

Ex. A. Hello, I'm looking for a warm sweater.
    B. How about this green one made in Scotland?

1. A. Which sport jacket should I wear to the interview?
    B. How about the one Uncle George gave you for your birthday?

2. A. Should I get the black tie or the blue one?
    B. Why don't you get the blue one?

3. A. Could I see the pocket-size camera in the leather case?
    B. Sure. Here it is. It's very inexpensive.

4. A. Which flag is the Japanese flag?
    B. It's the white one with the red sun in the middle.

5. A. Which dress should I wear to the party?
    B. How about this purple one made in France?

6. A. Why don't you have the pie that Aunt Helen usually orders?
    B. You mean the one with the apples and raisins in it?

7. A. Yes, that's the one.
    B. I think I will.

Page 20

Ex. Have you by any chance ever been to Taiwan?
1. Can you tell me what it's like in New York City?
2. It's one of the most exciting places I know.
3. Can you tell me anything else?
4. What else would you like to know?
5. How are the people and the beaches?
6. As far as I'm concerned, you'll have a fantastic time there.
7. In my opinion, China is a beautiful place.
8. As a matter of fact, you're right.
9. If you ask me, the people there are very friendly.
10. It sounds like a wonderful place.

Page 26

Ex. Arthur was fired, _____?
1. They predicted rain for tomorrow, _____?
2. Class is almost over, _____?
3. You'll be here on time, _____?
4. You haven't forgotten about it, _____?
5. You didn't read the wrong assignment, _____?
6. You've heard of him, _____?
7. You're not leaving, _____?
8. You won't be late, _____?

Page 27

Ex. They're going to build a school across the street?! She's just been promoted.
1. I'm going to get a raise?!
2. The mayor is coming to my office today.
3. The neighbors bought a new car?!
4. You're going out of business?!
5. I overheard a funny story.
6. There's a rumor going around about me?!
7. Our supervisor has resigned?!
8. He's absolutely sure.
9. You're fired.
10. I'm fired?!

Page 30

Ex. A. Excuse me, but would you mind turning down your radio? I'm trying to study.
    B. I'm sorry. I didn't hear you. What did you say?

1. A. Please open your books to page thirty-two.
    B. I'm sorry. I didn't hear that. Would you mind repeating that?

2. A. Put your bags down. I'll carry them.
    B. I'm sorry. What did you say?

3. A. Order an ice cream soda. They're delicious here.
    B. I'm sorry. I missed that. What should I order?

4. A. Why don't you change the station on the TV?
    B. Excuse me? Would you say that again?

5. A. Hand me a wrench, please. I want to put on this tire.
    B. Sure. Here it is.

6. A. Please turn down your stereo. I'm trying to sleep.
    B. I'm sorry. What did you say?

7. A. Turn right at the fourth light. Then, take your third left.
    B. I'm sorry. I didn't quite catch that.

8. A. Please get me a copy of this report.
    B. I'm sorry. What did you say? I didn't hear you.

9. A. Could you get me a hamburger and some french fries, please?
    B. Excuse me? What did you want?

Page 32

Ex. A. Can you tell me how to get to the bank?
B. Sure. Walk two blocks down Main Street and turn left. The bank is on the left.
Where is the bank?

1. A. Do you by any chance know where the station is?
B. Yes. Walk down Main Street three blocks, take a left, and the station is on the right at the end of the first block.
A. Thanks very much.
Where is the station?

2. A. Could you possibly tell me where the bus stop is?
B. I think so. Take your first left, walk to the corner, and the bus stop will be on your right.
Where is the bus stop?

3. A. Would you be able to tell me where Star Market is?
B. Sure. Walk to the corner of Main and Central Street, take a left, and follow Central for two blocks. Turn left and the market is the first building on the right.
A. Thank you.
Where is the market?

4. A. Let me see if I understand. I go to Beach, turn left, and take a right on Ivy. The drug store is at the end of the block on the left. Right?
B. That's right.
Where is the drug store?

5. A. Do you know where the police station is?
B. Uh-húh. Walk down Main Street to Beach. Follow Beach one block. Cross Ivy Street and the police station is on the left.
A. Thanks.
Where is the police station?

6. A. Can you tell me where Herman's Department Store is?
B. Sure. Go down Main to Central and take a left. Take a right on Lake and then your first left. Herman's is down the block on the left.
Where is Herman's?

Page 36

Ex. Could you possibly tell me where Main Street is?
1. Walk two blocks and turn right. Have you got it?
2. Let me see. I turn right and then left?
3. First, pick up the receiver and put in the money.
4. Would you possibly be able to direct me to the nearest post office?
5. Then, you mix these ingredients together. Are you with me so far?
6. Add the sugar to the butter, mix in some vanilla, then put the mixture aside. Okay?
7. Add oil, vinegar, spices, and a little wine. Did you get all of that?
8. Form the bread into a long loaf. Okay so far?

Page 37

Ex. First, put in one teaspoon of coffee. Then, add boiling water and stir.
1. First, put in thirty-five cents. Then, make your selection and the candy will drop out of the machine.
2. First, press eject. Then, put in the tape. Then, press play.
3. First write the date, then the name of the store and the amount of the purchase. Finally, sign your name.
4. First, unlock the door. Then, turn off the alarm. Then, start the ignition.
5. First, look through the lens. Then focus, and finally, push the button.
6. First, unscrew the old bulb. Then, get a new one and screw it into the lamp.

Page 38

Ex. A. That was some performance!
B. Thanks.

1. A. That was an excellent steak!
B. Yes, I thought it was superb.

2. A. Your lecture was wonderful.
B. Thanks for saying so.

3. A. Your presentation was absolutely fabulous!
B. Thank you. It's nice of you to say that.

4. A. That was some game!
B. Thank you.

5. A. Those photographs in your front hall are magnificent!
B. Thank you for saying so.

6. A. That was some concert. You were terrific!
B. It's nice of you to say that.

7. A. That was a very good report you gave on American farms.
B. Thank you.

8. A. That was a great picture you drew.
B. Thanks. It's nice of you to say that.

Page 38

Ex. A. Emily is a wonderful student.
B. Oh, I'm so glad to hear that.

1. A. I'm happy to tell you you're in excellent health.
B. That's great. Thanks.

2. A. You did very well on your test.
B. That's terrific. I was worried.

3. A. Am I really going to get that raise?
B. Yes. Absolutely.

4. A. I'm going to have to give you a ticket.
B. Oh, no!

5. A. The service was superb!
B. Thank you, sir.

6. A. Are you sure you're innocent?
B. Absolutely.

7. A. You did a fabulous job cleaning your room.
B. Thanks.

8. A. I have a magnificent house to show you.
B. Oh, that's great.

Page 43

1. I'd like one that's not too firm, but not too soft either.
2. Do you have one that's not so heavy?
3. This isn't long enough.
4. These are too bulky.
5. Is this too tight?
6. I wouldn't want it any shorter.
7. Don't you have an easier one?
8. These aren't warm enough?

Page 45

Ex. The movie wasn't as good as I thought it would be.
1. To tell you the truth, I was disappointed with my grades.
2. To be honest with you, I thought it was terrible.
3. I really hoped the class wouldn't be so long.
4. The waterfalls weren't as exciting as I had expected.
5. To be honest with you, Helen was nicer than I thought she would be.
6. How come you were disappointed?
7. Linda's presentation was more interesting than I thought it would be.
8. John's tennis partner was more challenging than he had expected him to be.
9. Well, honestly, the company was a little disappointed with Brian's work.
10. The baseball player wasn't very pleased with the score of the game.

Page 47

Ex. A. How about seeing a science fiction movie tonight?
B. Well, to tell you the truth, I don't like science fiction movies very much. How about a western?

1. A. How about Chinese food tonight?
B. Oh, I'm tired of Chinese food.

2. A. Let's go skating today.
B. Sure. That sounds good.

3. A. We could go sailing later.
B. Oh, I'm afraid I don't enjoy sailing.

4. A. I guess you must be tired of going bicycling.
B. No. On the contrary, I'd love to go bicycling.

5. A. Would you be interested in going dancing tonight?
B. Well, I'm not really crazy about dancing.

6. A. One of my favorite places to go for ice cream is Charlie's.
B. To tell you the truth, I'm really sick of ice cream.

7. A. Let's go to a fancy restaurant tonight.
B. Great!

8. A. If you don't like Indian food, we can go somewhere else.
B. No. I love Indian food.

9. A. Then it's settled. We'll leave at eight o'clock.
   B. Well, how about nine thirty?
10. A. Why don't we go hiking?
    B. Well, I'm afraid I don't particularly care for heights!

Page 54

Ex. A. Where do you want to go to dinner after this class?
    B. Oh, I don't care.

1. A. Here's the waiter. What kind of pizza should we order?
   B. Oh, it doesn't matter to me.
2. A. Would you like me to wrap up this plant for you or do you want to take it the way it is?
   B. I don't know. It's all the same to me.
3. A. Where do you want me to put the desk?
   B. It doesn't make any difference. I guess right here is okay.
4. A. Which wine should we order with our meal?
   B. I don't have any preference.
5. A. It's getting late and I'm tired. When do you want to leave this party?
   B. Oh, I don't care.
6. A. Let's order. How do you like your steak?
   B. I don't care. It's all the same to me.
7. A. Where do you want me to put these reports?
   B. It doesn't make any difference. Over there is fine.
8. A. What color should we paint this basement?
   B. I don't really have any preference.

Page 56

Ex. I guess I'd rather have the tomato soup.
1. Today we're featuring a choice of fresh vegetables or salad with the meal.
2. Would you like to order now?
3. I'd like to have some rolls and butter, please.
4. I'll have a glass of white wine, please.
5. Let me see . . . I think I'll order the special.
6. I'd prefer dark meat rather than white meat.
7. That's quite a selection! What would you recommend?
8. Would you care to have an appetizer?
9. The meal comes with salad, whether or not you order the special.
10. Which dressing would you rather have, French or Italian dressing?

Page 61

Ex. A. I promise I'll return the car by five o'clock.
    B. Okay. You don't have to hurry home.

1. A. You can count on me to do a good job.
   B. Good. We can use dependable people here at Westwood Medical Supply Company.
2. A. I promise we'll have these clothes ready for you by next Wednesday.
   B. Thanks. I'll pick them up then.
3. A. Can I count on you to write me often, dear?
   B. Sure. I won't let you down.
4. A. Will the pizza be ready soon? We have theater tickets and we don't want to be late.
   B. Definitely! I assure you it won't be more than a few more minutes.
5. A. Will we take off on time?
   B. Absolutely. Our flight will be right on time.
6. A. I'm relying on you to bring back my typewriter before my next paper is due.
   B. Don't worry. I guarantee it'll be back by tomorrow night.
7. A. Will the test be very difficult?
   B. I give you my word it won't be too difficult for you.
8. A. Now remember, I'm depending on you to close up the shop by six o'clock tonight.
   B. Don't worry. I'll take care of everything.

Page 65

Ex. Hi. It's me.
1. Tell me, what are you doing this afternoon?
2. Well, I'm planning to go skiing today. Would you be interested in joining me?
3. Where are you going next weekend?
4. If it's okay with you, I'll pick you up at six o'clock.
5. I'm going to run in the marathon.
6. I've made a big decision.

Page 67

Ex. A. What are you going to do tonight?
    B. I'm not sure. I might go to a movie.

1. A. Have you decided where to go for vacation?
   B. I'll probably go to Bermuda.
2. A. What are you going to order?
   B. Well, I thought I might try the scrambled eggs. I'm not sure yet.
3. A. Are you going to study English or German next semester?
   B. I may study English. I'm having a hard time deciding.
4. A. Are you going to ask for a raise?
   B. Absolutely!
5. A. I heard you're going to start your own business.
   B. Well, I've given it a lot of thought, and I've decided it's time to do it.
6. A. Which science course are you going to take?
   B. I'll most likely take Biology.
7. A. When are you going to retire?
   B. Well, I thought I'd stay one more year. I'm still thinking about it.
8. A. How are you going to pay for this suit?
   B. I'm going to charge it.
9. A. Where are you going to buy your calculator?
   B. I'm almost sure I'll get it at my friend's store on South Street.
10. A. What kind of dog are you going to get?
    B. I may get a terrier. Then again, I might get a poodle.

Page 67

1. I thought I might make an apple pie for dessert.
2. I'm thinking about taking Chinese.
3. I thought I'd make my father a sweater for his birthday.
4. I may go home early today.
5. I've been thinking of asking Ruth to the prom.
6. I might change my career soon.

Page 70

Ex. A. Do you want me to erase the board?
    B. No. That's okay. I don't mind erasing it.

1. A. Mrs. Crawford, I'll turn off all the lights if you'd like.
   B. Okay. I'd appreciate that, Sally.
2. A. I don't mind driving to work today, Bob.
   B. No, that's all right, Mike. I like driving.
3. A. Judy, let me feed the baby for a change. You're always the one who feeds the baby.
   B. Okay. Thanks. That would be nice, Richard.
4. A. John, wouldn't you like me to go grocery shopping?
   B. No. Don't worry about it, Linda. I don't mind going shopping.
5. A. I'd be glad to write that memo, if you'd like, Mr. Jones.
   B. No, that's okay. I don't mind writing it, Jack.

Page 71

Ex. I see you're cleaning out the attic. Do you want any help?
1. Lisa, do you need any help carrying those groceries?
2. Charlie, I see you're changing your snow tires. Need any help?
3. Would you mind helping me sweep out the garage?
4. Here, let me dry some of those dishes.
5. Larry, can I give you a hand with those skis?
6. My house hasn't been painted in a long time, so I thought I'd paint it this weekend.
7. Oh, no! My car is stuck in the snow!
8. Mr. Thompson, I'd be happy to finish up those technical drawings for you.

Page 72

Ex. Would you like me to carry those books for you, Fred?
1. I'd be glad to help you adjust the position of that picture.
2. Oh, thanks for offering, but I don't need any help.
3. Look! I insist! You're not cleaning the basement by yourself!
4. Well, okay. You can help, but I really don't want to put you to any trouble.
5. Oh, it's no trouble at all. I'm happy to lend you a hand.
6. There's no sense in your chopping all those carrots by yourself.

Ex. A. Hello. May I help you?
   B. Yes. I'm looking for a food processor for my father. He loves to cook, and it's his birthday tomorrow.
   A. I'm afraid we're out of food processors.
   B. Oh, that's too bad!
   A. But we expect some in by next week.
   B. Hmm. I'm afraid that's too late. I need it by tomorrow. Thanks anyway.
   What was the customer looking for?

1. A. Patty, do you want me to walk the dog?
   B. No. Don't worry about it, Frank. I don't mind walking the dog. I like the exercise.
   A. Listen! You're always the one who walks the dog. Let me, for a change.
   B. Well, okay. Thanks. It's nice of you to offer.
   Why does Frank want to walk the dog?

2. A. Hi, Vicky. I see you're planting your garden.
   B. Yes. It's time to put in the seeds.
   A. Well, can I give you a hand?
   B. Sure. If it's no trouble.
   A. No, not at all. I'd be happy to help. And anyway, I love being outside.
   B. Thanks. I appreciate that.
   Where did this conversation take place?

3. A. Joe, do you want me to help you lift those filing cabinets? They look pretty heavy.
   B. No, that's okay, Rick. I think I can move them myself. Each one only weighs about fifty pounds.
   A. Oh, come on, Joe. Let me give you a hand. You shouldn't have to move those by yourself if I'm here to help.
   B. Really, thanks for offering, but . . .
   A. Come on! I insist! You're not moving those by yourself.
   B. Well, okay. But I don't want to bother you.
   A. Joe, it's no trouble at all. Really, I'd be glad to help.
   How much does each filing cabinet weigh?

4. A. Hello. Can I help you?
   B. Yes. I'm looking for a Flexible Flyer sled.
   A. Oh, I'm afraid we don't have any Flexible Flyers in stock anymore. I believe they've stopped making them.
   B. Oh. What a pity!
   A. Well, is there anything else I can help you with?
   B. I guess not, but thanks anyway.
   Why didn't the store have Flexible Flyers?

5. A. Can I assist you?
   B. Yes. I'm looking for a pair of brown leather shoes like these in size thirteen.
   A. Well, we have them in size thirteen, but we only have them in black. Would you like me to get them for you?
   B. Sure, I'd appreciate that.
   What is the salesperson going to show the customer?

6. A. Hi. May I help you?
   B. Yes. I'm looking for a pet for my child.
   A. Uh-húh . . . How old is he?
   B. He's six and a half.
   A. Well, we have fish, hamsters, dogs, and cats.
   B. Do you have any birds?
   A. No, I'm afraid we're out of birds, but we expect to get some in next week.
   B. Okay, I'll come back then.
   What animals did the pet store have in stock?

Ex. Is smoking cigarettes allowed here?
1. Are you allowed to pet the animals at the zoo?
2. Is using a dictionary permitted during the TOEFL test?
3. Are people allowed to walk on the grass here at the Public Garden?
4. Excuse me, sir. Do they permit hunting here in the mountains?
5. Is it okay to sleep on the beach overnight?
6. Pardon me. Are you allowed to climb on those rocks?
7. Do they permit the sale of alcohol on Sundays in this state?

8. Are you allowed to touch the sculptures at this exhibit?
9. Excuse me. Are people permitted to have picnics here?
10. Is eating allowed in the library?

Ex. A. Would you mind if I turned up the stereo?
   B. No, I wouldn't mind.

1. A. Would it bother you if I took a picture of the performance?
   B. No, not at all.

2. A. Is it all right with you if I make fish for dinner?
   B. By all means. That sounds great.

3. A. Do you mind if I try a new dive?
   B. No, of course not. Go right ahead.

4. A. Would it be all right with you if I took a vacation soon?
   B. Sure. It's fine with me.

5. A. I'd like to do a few tests on your husband if that's all right with you.
   B. It's all right with me. I don't think he'll object.

6. A. Would you object to our visiting a few of my former students on our honeymoon?
   B. No, I don't mind.

7. A. If you'd rather I didn't have a pet in the apartment, I won't.
   B. No, that's okay. It's fine with me.

8. A. Is it okay to use my dictionary on the test?
   B. Certainly. Be my guest!

Ex. A. Would you mind if I turned on the radio?
   B. Well. I'd rather you didn't. I'm trying to study.

1. A. Is chewing gum allowed at camp?
   B. I think so.

2. A. Would it be all right if I put away the puzzle you've been working on?
   B. Actually, I'd prefer it if you wouldn't.

3. A. Can I enter the laboratory without permission?
   B. I don't think so.

4. A. Would you object if I started eating before you? I'm starving!
   B. No. Go right ahead.

5. A. Do you mind if I take Johnny to the zoo after twelve o'clock?
   B. No, of course not.

6. A. Do they allow men on that floor of the dormitory?
   B. I don't believe so.

7. A. Could I please have an ice cream sundae?
   B. Certainly.

8. A. Would it be possible for me to skip class on Friday?
   B. No. We're having a quiz on Friday.

9. A. Is it all right if I use the telephone for a while?
   B. I suppose so.

10. A. Mark, may I borrow your new record?
    B. I guess so. Why not?

Ex. Wendy, could I ask you to carry these bags for me?
1. I'm afraid I can't cash your check without an authorization from the bank manager.
2. Did the bank give you a hard time about the loan?
3. Would you agree to my subletting this apartment?
4. Is it okay to make a fire in the fireplace?
5. I'm sorry. You're not supposed to bring pets into the building.
6. I should mention that you're not allowed to tell anyone about this project.
7. I'm sorry, Mr. Harris. I don't mean to give you "the runaround," but you'll have to go to another department for your refund.